The Wesley Prayer Challenge

The Wesley Prayer Challenge
21 Days to a Closer Walk with Christ

The Wesley Prayer Challenge

978-1-7910-0721-8
978-1-7910-0722-5 eBook

The Wesley Prayer Challenge Leader Guide

978-1-7910-0723-2
978-1-7910-0724-9 eBook

The Wesley Prayer Challenge DVD

978-1-7910-0725-6

CHRIS FOLMSBEE

The Wesley Prayer Challenge

21 DAYS TO A CLOSER WALK WITH CHRIST

Abingdon Press / Nashville

LIBRARY OF CONGRESS CONTROL NUMBER: **2020941645**

ISBN-13: 978-1-7910-0721-8

20 21 22 23 24 25 26 27 28 29 — 10 9 8 7 6 5 4 3 2 1

MANUFACTURED IN THE UNITED STATES OF AMERICA

For Gina, Megan, Drew, and Luke

*Thanks to the people of The United Methodist
Church of the Resurrection*

*Thanks to Tom A, George M III, Dan R, Marsh S,
Russ H, Dave M, Mark P, Mark B
for your investment into my life and ministry*

CONTENTS

FOREWORD

No other prayer, aside from the Lord's Prayer, has had a deeper impact on my life than what *The United Methodist Hymnal* calls, "A Covenant Prayer in the Wesleyan Tradition." Most people simply call it the "Wesley Covenant Prayer." I'm grateful Chris Folmsbee has prepared this excellent resource for pondering, praying, and practicing the Covenant Prayer. He's a great writer, thinker, and leader in Christian discipleship, and I know you'll find this book inspiring and helpful.

I first learned of the Wesley Covenant Prayer in college. When I read it, then prayed it, it immediately spoke to me. Over the next couple of years, I memorized it, and somewhere along the way, I began praying it every morning. As I wake each day, I slip to my knees next to my bed, lift up my hands, and offer a word of praise to God. I spend time thanking God, ask for God's forgiveness, pray for others, then yield myself to God. It is in this last part of my prayer time that I turn to the prayer Wesley encouraged Methodists to pray at their Watch Night services.

Every morning for almost thirty-five years, I've made this prayer *my* prayer. Often, I pray it just as it appears here in this book. Sometimes I shorten it to its most basic element, drawn from Isaiah's prayer to God, "I'm here; send me" (Isaiah 6:8) or, "I'm yours, Lord; use me today."

I've often pondered the fact that I prefer praying some parts of the prayer over others. I'm really good with these parts: "Put me to doing...let me be employed by you...exalted for you...let me be full...let me have all things." These are easy to pray.

The real test is in praying their counterparts: "Put me to suffering...let me be laid aside for you...brought low for you...let me be empty...let me have nothing." No, these are not so easy to pray.

I had someone write to me several years ago who had broken a limb. They said, "I don't think I want to pray this prayer anymore. What kind of prayer asks God to put us to suffering?!" I responded, "This prayer is not about asking God to make us suffer for the sake of suffering. There are times that doing God's will might involve sacrifice or suffering, and as we pray this prayer, we are saying, "Even if it is costly, I want to do your will, O Lord." This is what Jesus was praying in the garden of Gethsemane when he said, "Not my will, but thy will be done."

My life has been lived far more often on the doing, employed, exalted, full, all things side of the prayer. But occasionally, I've experienced suffering and sacrifice. I've had moments when I was brought low, or empty, or when I felt like—at least spiritually and emotionally—I had nothing left. In those moments, this prayer means even more to me.

The Covenant Prayer leads me to think about the disciples in Acts 5:41, where, after having been beaten by the authorities, "The apostles left the council rejoicing because they had been regarded as worthy to suffer disgrace for the sake of the name." I think of Paul and Silas singing hymns at midnight in that Philippian prison cell. They had been beaten and stripped naked and humiliated in front of the people of Philippi. But they had sought to faithfully preach and teach and do God's will and, somehow, they believed God would work through their pain and imprisonment too. This gave meaning and hope to their suffering.

Sometimes our suffering is just part of life—I think of a couple of emergency-room visits for a rupturing appendix and an angry gall bladder that needed to come out. I knew God didn't cause these things, but as I prayed this prayer in the emergency room, or in pre-op, I was asking God to use these circumstances to sanctify me and to shape my life, and to use me in these circumstances to express his love to those in the emergency room or operating room. The Covenant Prayer, with its idea of yielding everything to God and inviting God to use all circumstances in our lives, does bring meaning to our suffering.

But perhaps as important, when we're living on the doing, employed, exalted, full, all things side of life, this prayer reminds us that all of these moments are intended to be lived for God. We are "blessed to be a blessing." We give our successes to God, recognizing God is the ultimate source of all good things, and we look for ways that our actions, our employment, our influence, and our blessings may be used for the glory of God.

How grateful I am for this prayer, and grateful for Chris Folmsbee's invitation to see in it new insights. Here we have new ways not only to pray this prayer, but also to live it.

Adam Hamilton
Senior Pastor
The United Methodist Church of the Resurrection

INTRODUCTION

I was in college when I first came across the Wesley Covenant Prayer. I grew up in a church with reformed theological perspectives, so John and Charles Wesley and the Methodist movement were not talked about much in my youth. While doing some research for a paper in one of my theology classes—my second year of college, I think it was—I came across the Wesley Covenant Prayer and thought, *How in the world have I not ever heard this prayer before? Why has no one taught me this prayer?*

A few weeks later, I was attending a Methodist church with a friend of mine over winter break, and I read an announcement in his church bulletin for a *Wesley Covenant Prayer Service* on the first Sunday in January. I was already captivated by the prayer and, by this time, had developed a habit of using it as my Monday morning prayer—to get my week off to a good start. The concept of a Wesley Covenant Prayer Service was new to me, just like the prayer had been only a few short months earlier. I leaned over to my college buddy and said, "What is this?" and pointed to the Covenant Service announcement in the bulletin. "Oh, that," he said. "That's nothing. It's a boring service we have every year. I used to go when I was a kid. I haven't been in about five years." "Let's come back for it," I said. "Really?" he said.

A couple of weeks after I read the announcement, we drove the ninety or so minutes to his rural church on the first Sunday of the new year. We invited a few of our friends to join us. My friend promised them a home-cooked meal. There were a handful of people there—mostly older people—and the handful of us who packed the car, mainly for a free home-cooked meal. I could tell the pastor was very pleased to see us. He greeted us with a smile and welcomed us with a sweet invitation to let the prayer wash over us and fill our hearts with a renewed passion for God and others. I remember the pastor's welcome being nearly as impactful as the prayer service itself.

The service was simple. Simpler than I expected it to be, actually. I wasn't disappointed; I just imagined going into the experience that the service would be longer and have more moving parts, so to speak. We didn't even sing a hymn, it was so simple. I'm not positive that this was the exact order of worship, but it's close:

Welcome
Opening Prayer
Scripture Reading
Reading of Wesley Covenant Prayer
Confession
Homily
Blessing & Benediction

I was moved deeply by the service. In its simplicity, I experienced a profound sense of renewal, as was its purpose. I found new meaning in my understanding of what it means to be a Christian and my pursuit to be like Christ. The Wesley Covenant Prayer Service I experienced that day was one of just a few worship experiences that changed the trajectory of my life. Because of the commitment of that church's members to renew their faith together every year, and because of that particular pastor's warm greeting and invitation to be open to God's work in my soul that day, I am changed. I am grateful for that experience. That prayer service is a marker in my life. When I am struggling to remain faithful to my commitment to Christ, I think back to that day and I am served with a reminder of what it means to be a faithful follower of Jesus.

After college, I lost track of the Wesley Covenant Prayer for a while. It wasn't until I began attending the church I currently serve, The United Methodist Church of the Resurrection near Kanas City, that I was reacquainted with another Covenant Service and began to live into my once-formed habit of Monday prayer.

For a decade, I have wanted to write this book—to give people a chance to either meet the prayer for the very first time or to be re-introduced to the prayer so that an experience of renewal might help lead them toward becoming a deeply committed disciple of Jesus. The daily reflections presented here are my attempts to interpret and break down the prayer into bite-sized portions for simpler contemplation and integration. As you will discover, my understanding of the Wesley Covenant Prayer goes beyond an individual prayer and emphasizes a communal sense of renewal. Through this, we understand the church as the primary agency that God is stirring to call its people to participate with God to restore the world toward its intended wholeness.

Before we go any further, let's take a moment to read the prayer. You may want to come back to the introduction so that you might reflect on the daily commentary within the context of the whole prayer. Here is the traditional version of the prayer:

I am no longer my own, but thine.
Put me to what thou wilt, rank me with whom thou wilt.
Put me to doing, put me to suffering.
Let me be employed by thee or laid aside for thee,
exalted for thee or brought low for thee.
Let me be full, let me be empty.
Let me have all things, let me have nothing.
I freely and heartily yield all things
to thy pleasure and disposal.
And now, O glorious and blessed God,
Father, Son, and Holy Spirit,
thou art mine, and I am thine. So be it.
And the covenant which I have made on earth,
let it be ratified in heaven. **Amen.**

Over the next twenty-one days, or however you choose to make your way through this book, I pray that you'll experience the peace and calming that so many have experienced over the years. Whether you choose this journey on your own or with a group (which I think is a very powerful way), I pray that you'll be stirred to renew and recommit your life to Christ. I pray that this renewal and recommitment will draw others to God's love as you faithfully attempt to live as the prayer guides you. This prayer, if you let it, will wreck your life. There is a very good chance that this prayer will change your perspective and your worldview. In fact, I would almost guarantee that if you open your heart and mind, and your hands for God's work, you'll never be the same again.

As you faithfully engage the principles and precepts in this prayer, they will change you, and hopefully those around you. The prayer is a call to discipleship; it is a call toward Christian perfection, or a total love for God and others. This prayer, deeply rooted in God's intended ways of life we see so clearly expressed in Jesus, is meant to demolish all of our immorality and, in its place, produce lifelong fruit. In the end, I pray that each of us will have a heart so full of God's holy love that there isn't room for anything else.

The Wesley Covenant Prayer was not actually original to John Wesley. Richard Alleine's prayer *A Vindiciae Pietatis* or *Vindication of Godliness* was the impetus for what we refer to as the Wesley Covenant Prayer as John Wesley adapted it for the first ever Covenant Service in August of 1755. The first covenant service is said to have had more than 1,800 people in attendance. Wesley is quoted to have said, "Such a night I scarce ever saw before. Surely the fruit of it shall remain for ever." From August of 1755 until now, the Covenant Service has been adapted, revised, and customized to meet the needs of congregations around the world.

This prayer is a means of grace and is meant for the Holy Spirit to empower our progress in our salvation. This salvific way, then, is meant to shape the behaviors of our life, enacting justice for the oppressed and producing an everyday kindness with which we love our neighbor with the same passion in which Jesus loves us. If the gospel is God's will, way, and work of providing salvation and justice for all, then we are leaving things undone if we merely see this prayer as a personal, internal aid to our own holiness. This prayer, to be in keeping with the life of Christ and Wesleyan theology, must be seen as a prayer for us *and* for the sake of the other.

I believe God's will is that the world be made whole. God's way of making the world whole is through the person and work of Jesus. God's work is done through the church, you and me, accepting our calling to be the light and to live out our salvation in a way that reminds the lonely, anxious, seeking, exploring, wondering world that God has not forgotten them. For the Wesley Covenant Prayer to be what I believe Wesley intended for it to be, it must change our lives and the lives of others.

If you'd like to renew your commitment to Christ, this book is for you. As you engage it, take seriously the intentions of the Wesley Covenant Prayer and integrate those intentions into your life, turning them into realities, and you'll be amazed at the fruit God produces within you that impacts the world around you. God bless you as you dig deep and work toward a closer walk with Christ.

PART ONE

SURRENDER AND SUFFERING

PART ONE

SURRENDER AND SUFFERING

Two concepts that are in conflict with most people's intended way of life are surrender and suffering. Many people I know are spirited, bring-it-on, and get-it-done kinds of people whose disposition is not to surrender or to cease resistance but instead to fight, particularly for their own rights or their perceived rights. In addition, most of the people I know well are wired to contest each struggle, battle, obstacle, conflict, or opposition they directly or indirectly encounter.

Regarding suffering, few of us want to think about the worst-case scenarios that might move us toward or take us into the middle of an enduring state of unhappiness, distress, turmoil, or pain of any kind. When we think of those who suffered in the Bible, we are reminded of Job who lost everything, Joseph who was sold as a slave, John the Baptist who was beheaded for his beliefs, Jesus, of course, who paid the ultimate price for the sake of the world, and his mom Mary, who suffered the loss of her son in a most dreadful way. To suffer is to undergo some sort of pain as a result of circumstances, sometimes but not always out of our control. Heartache and heartbreak are often associated with the pain we experience when we suffer.

These two words, *surrender* and *suffering*, are concepts most of us deliberately hope to sidestep. Wesley, however, in his proclamation and advancement of the Covenant Prayer, wishes us to think about surrender and suffering in a new kind of way. Surrender, in Wesley's mind, I believe, is to cease any and all resistance to God's will and way and wholeheartedly submit to God's authority and, therefore, do God's work in the world. Knowing the human condition is bent toward the consistent struggle to trust in ourselves and what we can control, Wesley endorses quite the opposite in the prayer. Wesley endorses letting go of control, whether real or perceived, and giving way to God's purposes for our lives.

To be clear, giving way is not giving up. Giving way is the mindful effort and deliberate action to yield to God's will, which, said one way, is to participate in God's mission to restore the world toward its intended wholeness. Giving up is the exact opposite. In fact, to give up is void of any effort or action altogether. There is no physical action required to give up. To give up is simply to quit. Obviously, Wesley does not intend for Christians to quit. Wesley intends for Christians to seek first God's will by becoming wholly devoted to God's mission.

In a similar way, Wesley understands that to suffer is to subject ourselves to God's will, even as far as the extremes of loss, inconvenience, misery, grief, and acute pain may take us. To suffer for God's will is to embrace the unpleasantness of life, regardless of how intolerable it might be, how frequent it might be, or how long or short of a time it might be. Christians who surrender to God's will cannot fully surrender without also realizing that bearing hardship of any kind, especially for the sake of others, might be inevitable and even necessary.

To surrender, even at the cost of whatever suffering it may cause, is to wholeheartedly and totally give ourselves to God and God's mission. Deeply committed disciples give way to God's will, way, and work, and embrace the image and likeness in which we've been created. This movement toward becoming fully human means that Christians must embrace and endorse what it means to surrender *to* God and suffer *for* God. Together, we'll take the next seven days to explore what it means to completely dedicate ourselves to participating in God's mission to restore the world to its intended wholeness.

DAY ONE

"I AM..."

Today's Scripture Reading

At one time you were like a dead person because of the things you did wrong and your offenses against God. You used to live like people of this world. You followed the rule of a destructive spiritual power. This is the spirit of disobedience to God's will that is now at work in persons whose lives are characterized by disobedience. At one time you were like those persons. All of you used to do whatever felt good and whatever you thought you wanted so that you were children headed for punishment just like everyone else.

However, God is rich in mercy. He brought us to life with Christ while we were dead as a result of those things that we did wrong. He did this because of the great love that he has for us. You are saved by God's grace! And God raised us up and seated us in the heavens with Christ Jesus. God did this to show future generations the greatness of his grace by the goodness that God has shown us in Christ Jesus.

You are saved by God's grace because of your faith. This salvation is God's gift. It's not something you possessed. It's not something you did that you can be proud of. Instead, we are God's accomplishment, created in Christ Jesus to do good things. God planned for these good things to be the way that we live our lives.

Ephesians 2:1-10

Reflection

The first two words of Wesley's prayer are inextricably linked and undeniably essential to understanding the prayer in its entirety. Without a profound examination into the words *I am*, we may potentially dismiss the prayer as distant and vague or perhaps even determine that the prayer is meant for others, not us. When in actuality, the words *I am* can only be seen as deeply personal.

Wesley's prayer demands that we associate the prayer with us, personally. This does not mean the prayer is void of a shared or communal aspect; it certainly is. Rooted deeply within the communal commitment to enact the prayer, however, is a personal and intimate expression of self, "I am."

To some, the words *I am* may seem regular or ordinary. However, the words are extraordinary, for they convey that we, all human beings, are created in the image and likeness of God. Without God's intentional act of love—creating us each uniquely, yet connected to others through spiritual and emotional understanding, physical resemblance, and social relationships—we are merely matter void of purpose and meaning. However, each of us is, in fact, deliberately created with purpose and meaning.

One way to think about purpose and meaning is to think about purpose as our reason for being, objectively. Meaning, then, is the values and beliefs we associate with or assign to our reason for being, subjectively. In other words, purpose tells us who we have been created to be, and meaning tells us the significance and worth we find in the repetition of living out our purpose. When we live according to purpose and meaning, we find peace.

> # *When we live according to purpose and meaning, we find peace.*

For me, personally, purpose can be summed up in three primary reasons for my being. One reason for my being is simply to worship God. When I express my awe and love of God through prayer, fasting, song, attending church, studying Scripture, giving, serving others, or sharing my faith, I worship God. A second reason for my being is to represent God to all those I come into contact with, reminding them that God is a loving

God who has not forgotten them. This means that I am determined to fill my heart so full of love that there isn't room for anything else within it. When people come around me, my hope is that they sense a love for God and others. This love then compels them to explore God in meaningful ways. Finally, a third reason for my being is simply to help people become deeply committed disciples. This is why I serve as a discipleship director at my church and teach, mentor, organize small groups, and plan retreats, so that people can become more devoted to their faith through events, experiences, and environments that lead them down the pathway toward being deeply committed. If someone were to ask me, "What is your purpose?" I would respond simply by saying, "My reason for being is to worship God, love God and others daily, and to help people become deeply committed disciples of Jesus Christ."

I find meaning in my purpose when I have opportunity to feel and see that my purpose-driven efforts are working. When I feel inspired through worshipping God, I know I am living into my purpose. When I can help the people around me feel God's love, I know I am living into my purpose. When I watch people grow in their faith and develop an insatiable desire to learn more and practice more of the Christian faith, I find meaning and feel worth and significance. Simply said, when I live into my purpose or exercise the reason for my being, I find value, worth, and usefulness in my reason for being and it compels me to be more Christlike.

Therefore, to be created in the image and likeness of God, with purpose and meaning, is to be created for the reason of reflecting God's glory or to represent God. We represent God best when we understand that in "I am," we are spiritual, relational, and moral beings designed to present to the world around us the main subject of God, which is love.

We are spiritual beings in that we are people who reason, possess a will, and act with complete freedom: a freedom that allows us to love God (or not) by choosing to submit to God's ways. We are relational beings in that we have been created to be in community and to live in God's good creation with a longing for the well-being of all of God's creation, other human beings and the beautiful world around us. Finally, we are

Today's Challenge:

REPRESENT

Today, at least three times, within your sphere(s) of influence, choose the best method and course of action to represent God to others. The best way to do this might be to take action once in the morning, once in the afternoon, and once in the evening.

moral beings. This means that we are capable of knowing, loving, and serving God—to be filled so full of love, there isn't room for anything else in our being.

In the Wesleyan theological tradition, we call a heart so full of love that there isn't room for anything else "Christian perfection." This perfection is not a static state in which we live free from sin or any other flaw or defect, of course. Christian perfection is, however, the dynamic process of experiencing God's grace in which we are moving on to maturity. I like to describe this dynamic process as increasing the frequency and duration of the holy moments in our life. In other words, how often and for how long can I consistently express a love for God and others.

It is important that we do not move too swiftly or read too quickly past the first two words *I am*. In those two words, we find a rich and robust understanding of who we are and the worth that we find and possess in our being. Ultimately, Wesley wants us to know that God is love and, in that love, we are God's representatives of God's love. We ought to symbolize God's grace, mercy, and justice to all whom we come into contact with, wherever we live, work, study, or play. This means that wherever God has directed our paths, there we are intended to be an icon of God's great love for all of God's creation.

I encourage you to remember the Great "I Am," God, who in God's self-existent, eternal, and self-sufficient being is the source and sustainer of all of life and, therefore, is worthy of all worship and honor. We are alive because the Creator and Sustainer of life, the true source of existence, created us for a loving relationship with God and others.

Personal Reflection

- What is my purpose for life?
- Where do I find meaning for life?

Group Discussion

- In what ways do you best represent God to others?
- Based on today's commentary, how would you describe what it means to be created in the image and likeness of God?
- Describe the specifics of your spheres of influences. (Think: places in your life where you have an opportunity to make an impact.)
- What would you say is the main idea of this part of the prayer?

Departing Prayer

God, help us to remember who we are and whose we are—and to represent you as an emblem of love wherever we live, work, study, or play. Amen.

DAY TWO

"...NO LONGER MY OWN,"

Today's Scripture Reading

The snake was the most intelligent of all the wild animals that the LORD God had made. He said to the woman, "Did God really say that you shouldn't eat from any tree in the garden?"

The woman said to the snake, "We may eat the fruit of the garden's trees but not the fruit of the tree in the middle of the garden. God said, 'Don't eat from it, and don't touch it, or you will die.'"

The snake said to the woman, "You won't die! God knows that on the day you eat from it, you will see clearly and you will be like God, knowing good and evil." The woman saw that the tree was beautiful with delicious food and that the tree would provide wisdom, so she took some of its fruit and ate it, and also gave some to her husband, who was with her, and he ate it. Then they both saw clearly and knew that they were naked. So they sewed fig leaves together and made garments for themselves.

During that day's cool evening breeze, they heard the sound of the LORD God walking in the garden; and the man and his wife hid themselves from the LORD God in the middle of the garden's trees. The LORD God called to the man and said to him, "Where are you?"

The man replied, "I heard your sound in the garden; I was afraid because I was naked, and I hid myself."

He said, "Who told you that you were naked? Did you eat from the tree, which I commanded you not to eat?"

The man said, "The woman you gave me, she gave me some fruit from the tree, and I ate."

The LORD God said to the woman, "What have you done?!"

And the woman said, "The snake tricked me, and I ate."

The LORD God said to the snake,

> "Because you did this,
>> you are the one cursed
>>> out of all the farm animals,
>>> out of all the wild animals.
>> On your belly you will crawl,
>>> and dust you will eat
>>> *every day of your life.*

I will put contempt

>> between you and the woman,
>> between your offspring and hers.
> They will strike your head,
>> *but you will strike at their heels."*

To the woman he said,

> "I will make your pregnancy very painful;
>>> in pain you will bear children.
> You will desire your husband,
>> *but he will rule over you."*

To the man he said, "Because you listened to your wife's voice and you ate from the tree that I commanded, 'Don't eat from it,'

> cursed is the fertile land because of you;
>> in pain you will eat from it
>> every day of your life.
> Weeds and thistles will grow for you,
>> even as you eat the field's plants;
> by the sweat of your face you will eat bread—
>> until you return to the fertile land,
>>> since from it you were taken;
>>> you are soil,
>>>> to the soil you will return."

29

The man named his wife Eve because she is the mother of everyone who lives. The LORD God made the man and his wife leather clothes and dressed them. The LORD God said, "The human being has now become like one of us, knowing good and evil." Now, so he doesn't stretch out his hand and take also from the tree of life and eat and live forever, the LORD God sent him out of the garden of Eden to farm the fertile land from which he was taken. He drove out the human. To the east of the garden of Eden, he stationed winged creatures wielding flaming swords to guard the way to the tree of life.

Genesis 3

Reflection

When we pray the Wesley Covenant Prayer, we must recognize, as we discussed in the previous day's reflection, that we are created in the image and likeness of God. We are spiritual, moral, and relational beings, designed with purpose and designed to experience a life full of meaning. We are to reflect God's good way, which is to love all those we come into contact with or come into contact with us—wherever we might live, work, study, or play.

The second part of the prayer, moving beyond our self-revelation in the words *I am*, is the description, "no longer my own." In fact, as we all know, we were never really our own. We belong to God for God's purposes. This is the truth embedded in "I am." This admission, that we are God's and not our own, is often in direct conflict with the inner desire we harbor in our nature—to act independent of God's will. We face this conflict daily, sometimes multiple times a day.

For me, one thing immediately comes to mind: money. You may have heard this another time or two in your life, but John Wesley is credited with saying, "Earn all you can. Save all you can. Give all you can." Sometimes in my life, although I am better about this than I ever have been before, by the grace of God, I forget that Wesley's statement has two other key aspects beyond earning all I can. If I didn't practice automatic giving through electronic funds transfer, I could easily get offtrack and find it difficult to save and to give. Although, for me, giving is easier than saving because I find deep meaning in charitable actions.

> ## *"Earn all you can. Save all you can. Give all you can."*
> ## *– John Wesley*

Truthfully, like all of those around us, we struggle daily to turn our trust away from self and toward God. The freedom we have, having been created as beings with the ability to choose, is God's way of sharing God's love with us. God loves us so much that in that love, God gave us the ability to love God back, or not. This is the fundamental struggle within all of humanity—to love God and let God be the god of our life, or not.

The story of Adam and Eve in Genesis chapter 3 gives us a picture of what all humans are like. (Genesis chapters 1 and 2 give us a picture of what the world was like before the fall of humanity, let's not forget.) Distracted by and drawn toward what is "pleasing to the eye" (Genesis 3:6 NIV), Adam and Eve chose to exercise their freedom of will and, in doing so, usurped God's authority through the eating of the fruit. This self-centered action of eating the fruit from the tree of the knowledge of good and evil, from which they knew they were not to eat, was a deliberate action to do their own thing. Eating the fruit was a measured way of putting their trust in their own selves, their own understanding and reason, rather than in God's order.

The decision to disregard God's order, as you know, had tremendous implications for Adam and Eve. No longer were they allowed to live freely in paradise, in the garden of Eden; they were expelled from it. God, in God's amazing grace, continues to provide, protect, and love as only God can, but their life of peace and intimacy with God was now twisted with shame and blame. This shame and blame led to other self-interested wickedness and, over a period of time, God's heart was broken and God becomes sorry that God ever created human beings and put them on the earth. We know from Genesis 6:5-6, which says, "The LORD saw that humanity had become thoroughly evil on the earth and that every idea their minds thought up

Today's Challenge:
BE BOLD

Make a list of at least three struggles of self-interest that keep you from trusting in God more fully. Share the three struggles with family, friends, or others in your small group. Ask them to hold you accountable to purge them from your behavior or lifestyle.

was always completely evil. The LORD regretted making human beings on the earth, and he was heartbroken."

Christians who choose to surrender their own will and return to God's will live out the prayer that they are "no longer our own." Christians who faithfully do this are making a conscious effort and taking immediate action to let God's will and mission for this world be the prevailing purpose for their life. It is in that purpose where meaning is discovered and consistently experienced. The end of the story is not a broken world in which God is grieved that God created humans and put them on the earth. The end of the story (as we see in Revelation chapters 21 and 22) is paradise restored. The end of the story is actually the beginning of a new story, a new earth, that is marked by peace and wholeness as opposed to disharmony and brokenness. Our Christian hope projects the belief that, one day, the world will know no brokenness, only wholeness.

Revelation gives us a glimpse of a paradise restored:

> Then the angel showed me the river of life-giving water, shining like crystal, flowing from the throne of God and the Lamb through the middle of the city's main street. On each side of the river is the tree of life, which produces twelve crops of fruit, bearing its fruit each month. The tree's leaves are for the healing of the nations. There will no longer be any curse. The throne of God and the Lamb will be in it, and his servants will worship him. They will see his face, and his name will be on their foreheads. Night will be no more. They won't need the light of a lamp or the light of the sun, for the Lord God will shine on them, and they will rule forever and always.

> Revelation 22:1-5

The admission that "I am no longer my own" in Wesley's prayer gives us a new or renewed vision for our life, a vision of a paradise restored in which God dwells with God's people and one in which there is no more darkness, only the light of God. When we pray, "I am no longer my own," we resist the urge to have our individual desires and interests prevail. In their places, we surrender ourselves to God's good work of restoring the world toward its intended wholeness and work attentively to represent God with our entire lives.

Personal Refection

- If I am honest with myself, how do I answer the question, "Do I live as 'my own'?"
- With what three areas in my life do I have a hard time trusting God?

Group Discussion

- Do you agree with the author that a fundamental struggle for humanity is to love God by letting God be God and not trying to be or have our own gods? Why or why not?
- What distractions or items that are "pleasing to the eye" do you wrestle with?
- In what ways do you intentionally temper your individual desires or areas of self-interest?
- What would you say is the main idea of this part of the prayer?

Departing Prayer

Teach us to trust you, God. Help us to use our freedom of will to allow you to truly be the only God in our lives. Help us to resist what is "pleasing to the eye" so that your will might be done. Amen.

DAY THREE

"...BUT THINE."

Today's Scripture Reading

Now the boy Samuel was serving the LORD under Eli. The LORD's word was rare at that time, and visions weren't widely known. One day Eli, whose eyes had grown so weak he was unable to see, was lying down in his room. God's lamp hadn't gone out yet, and Samuel was lying down in the LORD's temple, where God's chest was.

The LORD called to Samuel. "I'm here," he said.

Samuel hurried to Eli and said, "I'm here. You called me?"

"I didn't call you," Eli replied. "Go lie down." So he did.

Again the LORD called Samuel, so Samuel got up, went to Eli, and said, "I'm here. You called me?"

"I didn't call, my son," Eli replied. "Go and lie down."

(Now Samuel didn't yet know the LORD, and the LORD's word hadn't yet been revealed to him.)

A third time the LORD called Samuel. He got up, went to Eli, and said, "I'm here. You called me?"

Then Eli realized that it was the LORD who was calling the boy. So Eli said to Samuel, "Go and lie down. If he calls you, say, 'Speak, LORD. Your servant is listening.'" So Samuel went and lay down where he'd been.

Then the LORD came and stood there, calling just as before, "Samuel, Samuel!"

Samuel said, "Speak. Your servant is listening."

The LORD said to Samuel, "I am about to do something in Israel that will make the ears of all who hear it tingle! On that day, I will bring to pass against Eli everything I said about his household—every last bit of it! I told him that I would punish his family forever because of the wrongdoing he knew about—how his sons were cursing God, but he wouldn't stop them. Because of that I swore about Eli's household that his family's wrongdoing will never be reconciled by sacrifice or by offering."

Samuel lay there until morning, then opened the doors of the LORD's house. Samuel was afraid to tell the vision to Eli. But Eli called Samuel, saying: "Samuel, my son!"

"I'm here," Samuel said.

"What did he say to you?" Eli asked. "Don't hide anything from me. May God deal harshly with you and worse still if you hide from me a single word from everything he said to you." So Samuel told him everything and hid nothing from him.

"He is the LORD," Eli said. "He will do as he pleases."

So Samuel grew up, and the LORD was with him, not allowing any of his words to fail.

1 Samuel 3:1-19

Reflection

In the previous two days, we've been motivated to reflect and take action on who we are and what it means to be no longer our own. Subsequently, let's say that we are ready to fully surrender ourselves to God and God's good, restoring work in the world. To whom and what, then, are we actually surrendering? If we are genuinely ready and willing to confront our own personal interests and desires and do the daily soul work required to make the effort of surrendering realized, then as we put down ourselves, what exactly are we picking up or taking on?

When we lay down our own interests and pick up God's will for the world, we are picking up God's mission. God's mission is God's loving action of restoring the world toward its intended wholeness, as we described in the

Today's Challenge:
PROXIMITY AND TIME

Intimacy in any relationship requires proximity and time. Set your alarm on your phone, watch, or other clock at the top of each hour from 9:00 a.m. through 9:00 p.m. At the top of each hour, as the alarm reminds you, spend two minutes talking with God, reading a verse, listening, writing a prayer, or another activity. At the end of the day, take five minutes to journal your experience.

preceding daily reflection. It is important for me to be clear that my intentional use of the words *toward* and *wholeness* is in an effort to make sure that I am not projecting the idea of going back to the way the world was in Eden. Instead, we are moving forward toward, or in the direction of, the way the world should be. This means that God desires for our world to be made whole, as it was at the time of Creation, and that is where God is taking us. God's will is that the world would be made whole. God's way of making that a reality, a peace-filled, harmonious world, is through the life, death, burial, resurrection, and ascension of Jesus. God's work to make the world whole is done through the universal church living out the practices of Jesus, as empowered and guided by the Holy Spirit.

It might be said that God the Father sends God the Son, God the Son sends God the Spirit, and God the Spirit sends the church into the world. Perhaps this is the shortest way to understand and articulate the meta-narrative of the Bible. God is a missionary God, a sending God, who calls the Church, local and global, to participate with God in the mission and then sends the Church to accomplish the work. I believe that acceptance of this mission or to realize that "I am no longer my own, but Thine" requires faithful participation in God's mission to grow toward deep levels of intimacy, vulnerability, and dependency.

To admit that we belong to God (or to say, "but thine") is to declare God as *Abba* Father. This means that we have a closeness or togetherness, a deep familiarity with God. In the New Testament, Jesus refers to God as "Abba" in Mark 14:36 while praying in the garden of Gethsemane hours before his death. *Abba* is an Aramaic term meaning "father" that denotes the special intimacy of a father-son relationship. Intimacy means total life-sharing. Intimacy is a closeness or oneness either emotionally, physically, or socially that requires at least two key factors. These two factors are proximity and time. Proximity is nearness to another, and time is, of course, the instances in which we share life with God.

Vulnerability is opening up our lives in such a way as to expose our true self before God and others. To claim, "but thine" is, therefore, to invite God and God's will into our lives, knowing that we are people in need of God's redemption. Said differently, to pray, "but thine," is to admit the need for a redeemer and then living daily knowing that God's gracious gift of God's Son, Jesus, as the Lord and Savior of the world, is where we find abundant life. When we live vulnerable Christian lives, we live knowing that we are opening ourselves up to what we've discovered we need most—redemption. By being vulnerable in this way, and linking to God's mission, we are also putting ourselves in a position that could create inconvenience or even harder, more difficult positions of pain and suffering for the sake of the world. This is why, I believe, so many people struggle with intimacy with God, because it requires us to be vulnerable. And, in being vulnerable, completely or wholly vulnerable, we'd have to welcome the possibility of unwelcome and unwanted situations and circumstances in our lives.

> *When we live vulnerable Christian lives, we live knowing that we are opening ourselves up to what we've discovered we need most— redemption.*

Finally, as participants with God in God's mission, we strive for a deep level of dependency upon God. Through intimacy and vulnerability, we choose to persistently place our lives in God's hands, trusting God for our every need—spiritually, emotionally, relationally, financially, and so forth. To depend on God is to live with a bias of hope that God is who God says God is. To live with dependence on God is to trust the mission of God. To live with dependence is to trust that the will, way, and work of God is true and active. Because of a commitment to those beliefs, it produces within us a confident expectation that in our work, no matter how overwhelming or daunting it may be, God's will for a whole world will prevail and all things will one day be made new.

Personal Reflection

- On a scale of 1–10, 10 being no room for improvement, how fully surrendered am I to doing God's good work in the world?
- Do I spend daily quality time with God, and do I readily admit that I am grateful for the gift of redemption?

Group Discussion

- How would you describe God's will?
- In what ways is God a missionary God?
- Where do you find your "substance" for life?
- What does it mean to depend on God?
- What would you say is the main idea of this part of the prayer?

Departing Prayer

Guide us into holiness as we seek to draw near to you, share our lives with you, and learn to more deeply depend on you for all of our needs. Amen.

DAY FOUR

"PUT ME TO WHAT THOU WILT,"

Today's Scripture Reading

So we try to persuade people, since we know what it means to fear the Lord. We are well known by God, and I hope that in your heart we are well known by you as well. We aren't trying to commend ourselves to you again. Instead, we are giving you an opportunity to be proud of us so that you could answer those who take pride in superficial appearance, and not in what is in the heart.

If we are crazy, it's for God's sake. If we are rational, it's for your sake. The love of Christ controls us, because we have concluded this: one died for the sake of all; therefore, all died. He died for the sake of all so that those who are alive should live not for themselves but for the one who died for them and was raised.

So then, from this point on we won't recognize people by human standards. Even though we used to know Christ by human standards, that isn't how we know him now. So then, if anyone is in Christ, that person is part of the new creation. The old things have gone away, and look, new things have arrived!

All of these new things are from God, who reconciled us to himself through Christ and who gave us the ministry of reconciliation. In other words, God was reconciling the world to himself through Christ, by not counting people's sins against them. He has trusted us with this message of reconciliation.

So we are ambassadors who represent Christ. God is negotiating with you through us. We beg you as Christ's representatives, "Be reconciled to God!" God caused the one who didn't know sin to be sin for our sake so that through him we could become the righteousness of God.

2 Corinthians 5:11-21

Reflection

We are advancing nicely through part one of Wesley's prayer. On day one, we started with acknowledging that we are created in the image of God and with an understanding of what it means to have purpose and meaning in our lives. Day two, we progressed toward learning what it means to wholly surrender ourselves to God's good work in the world. Day three, we briefly yet broadly outlined what God's good work in the world is—a world restored. Now, here on day four, we are going to identify the kinds of actions God might require of us in order to live on mission, or to faithfully participate with God to restore the world toward its intended wholeness.

Wesley's prayer now guides us into action—"Put me to what thou wilt" is a way of saying, "Use me for whatever you need, God." Once we realize who we are and for what we have been created, we can begin to see that within God's good, redemptive work in the world we play a vital role. We are the agents of reconciliation or the ambassadors that God is using to draw people toward God. Second Corinthians 5:20 says, "…we are ambassadors who represent Christ. God is negotiating with you [the church in Corinth] through us [those who believe]." This is part of God's plan of grace. Wesleyans refer to this type of grace as *prevenient grace*. Prevenient grace is the grace God gives that is meant to prepare people's hearts in order to recognize and receive God's gift of salvation.

> *Prevenient grace is the grace God gives that is meant to prepare people's hearts in order to recognize and receive God's gift of salvation.*

Like a messenger sent to bring the good news to the people of Israel in the Isaiah passage below, so do we as faithful Christians, designed with purpose and for meaning, bring the good news to all those whom we come into contact with wherever we live, work, study, or play. Isaiah's words provide a great picture to see how we might be used of God as we are put to God's will:

How beautiful upon the mountains
    are the feet of a messenger
    who proclaims peace,
    who brings good news,
    who proclaims salvation,
    who says to Zion, "Your God rules!"
Listen! Your lookouts lift their voice;
    they sing out together!
Right before their eyes they see the LORD returning to Zion.

Break into song together, you ruins of Jerusalem!
The LORD has comforted his people and has redeemed Jerusalem.
The LORD has bared his holy arm in view of all the nations;
    all the ends of the earth have seen our God's victory.

Isaiah 52:7-10

We are the messengers that God wills. God directs and, as a result, faithful disciples respond submissively. Deeply committed disciples are to proclaim peace, bring good news, proclaim salvation, and shout (with word and deed) that God rules, God returns to God's people, and God redeems. We, the church, are the holy arm that God enlists to see victory. This means that we drop our own agendas and self-interests, and take on more humility and generosity for the sake of others, or as Jesus prays in John 17:23, so that "the world will know."

In Jesus's High Priestly Prayer (John 17:1-26), Jesus prays for three matters. First, he prays for himself that he might honor God in his submissive actions leading to death on the cross. Second, he prays for his friends, his disciples. Finally, Jesus prays for all future believers who will come to a belief in God's goodness because of the work his disciples will carry out after Jesus's resurrection and return to God's side. In essence,

Today's Challenge:
RANDOM KINDNESS

Make a list of three random acts of kindness that you can do today. Share them with others so that you are held accountable. Perform the acts of kindness and spend time reflecting on your experience.

Jesus prays for the sake of the world—that the world would know the love of God as Jesus knows the love of God. This is an incredible illustration of Jesus living the prayer, "Put me to what thou wilt."

Like Jesus, when we as Christians live for the sake of others, we take thoughtful action on allowing God to "Put me (us) to what thou wilt." This means, as you might imagine, that we are subject to God's authority, and when we receive a special calling or a Spirit-stimulated impression upon our mind or heart, we must take action upon it. How might God put us to what God wills? First, God might ask you, similarly to how he asked the prophet Jonah in the Old Testament, to take on a task that seems to human logic like a waste of time. Or, maybe, like Moses, God asks you to lead a group of people that is marked by defiance, constant grumbling, and rugged hearts. Paul was asked to take the gospel to unfamiliar places and literally put his life on the line when doing so. When God puts us to what God wills, God gives us a special assignment in which to participate in God's redemptive activity.

Second, God may ask you to do what appears to be the mundane with your special assignment. Maybe you aren't asked to put your life on the line and take the gospel into the unfamiliar as Paul did. Perhaps you are, however, asked to simply pray, listen, and care. Praying, "Put me to what thou wilt," may mean that you are called to pray for the sick, listen well to the stories of others, and care for others by meeting their needs. It may even mean that you are called to share your personal possessions with those in need, or invite people into your community who may not otherwise have a community in which to belong and feel safe.

Finally, to ask God to "Put me to what thou wilt" might mean that you are unusually stretched beyond your comfort zone and asked to do things like speak up and speak out to your friends, or even strangers, when you hear them speak with prejudice or discrimination. You may be asked to help develop more opportunities for people of color to lead in corporate, community, or church settings, or maybe even asked to protest or march for those oppressed by racism or any other of the many -isms afflicting our world today, such as classism, sexism, or ageism. "Put me to what thou wilt" may actually mean that you are putting your life on the line for the sake of others. Right now, as I write this, the COVID-19 pandemic is taking the world by storm. Doctors, nurses, first responders, people in the service industry, pastors, and others are quite literally putting their lives on the line each time they care for a person who may be a carrier of the coronavirus. We pray, "Put me to what thou wilt," knowing that God's plan for our life is not our plan, and that if we are faithful to the prayer, we lay down our own selves for the sake of the other. This is how God's kingdom works.

Personal Reflection

- How open am I to being put to God's work?
- Why have I been created? Am I living into that?

Group Discussion

- How do you understand prevenient grace?
- Where might God be sending you to bring good news?
- What are the ordinary areas of life God might be calling you to serve?
- What are the extraordinary areas of your life God might be calling you to serve?
- What would you say is the main idea of this part of the prayer?

Departing Prayer

Give us a clear picture of where we can be the messengers of God's good news. Give us compassionate hearts for others and grant us the courage to carry out any special assignments that God might have for us. Amen.

DAY FIVE

"...RANK ME WITH WHOM THOU WILT."

Today's Scripture Reading

And Jesus went to the Mount of Olives. Early in the morning he returned to the temple. All the people gathered around him, and he sat down and taught them. The legal experts and Pharisees brought a woman caught in adultery. Placing her in the center of the group, they said to Jesus, "Teacher, this woman was caught in the act of committing adultery. In the Law, Moses commanded us to stone women like this. What do you say?" They said this to test him, because they wanted a reason to bring an accusation against him. Jesus bent down and wrote on the ground with his finger.

They continued to question him, so he stood up and replied, "Whoever hasn't sinned should throw the first stone." Bending down again, he wrote on the ground. Those who heard him went away, one by one, beginning with the elders. Finally, only Jesus and the woman were left in the middle of the crowd.

Jesus stood up and said to her, "Woman, where are they? Is there no one to condemn you?"

She said, "No one, sir."

Jesus said, "Neither do I condemn you. Go, and from now on, don't sin anymore."

John 8:1-11

Reflection

I believe that this part of the prayer has mostly to do with our reputations—the beliefs or opinions that people hold about us. Each one of us desires to have a place of standing in society where we are measured by success, influence, intelligence, power, or achievement. Some of us want to be considered funny or hip. Some of us want to be considered important and impressive. Others want to be considered attractive and talented. Still others wish to be known for their wealth and prestige. Whatever it is, we all struggle to let go of control over manipulating our reputations. We care how we are perceived by others.

A few weeks ago, I was leading a meeting of discipleship pastors and directors in Denver, Colorado. We were discussing various ways to engage younger generations (specifically millennials and Gen Z) in discipleship using digital methods, such as apps and online tools. I had invited the attendees to the meeting, many of whom did not know each other or who knew of each other but had never personally met. One of the attendees, a friend and colleague whom I have known for over two decades, was in the room and seated next to me. We were having a casual conversation, when another person I had invited walked into the conference room. This person was immediately met by a small group of other attendees and engaged in conversation. My friend leaned over the table and said something like this: "You didn't tell me that *so-and-so* was going to be here. Had I known he was coming, I would have spent way more time on the design of the slides in my deck. I would have done more research, and I would have most definitely refined my presentation."

I clearly must have looked confused or puzzled because my friend looked me square in the eyes before I could respond and said, "What?! I want him to like me." I responded saying, "He's not going to like you less or more based off of your slides and your polished or unpolished presentation. He's going to like you less or more based on how true to yourself you actually are. Just be yourself."

Clearly, my friend wanted this person to leave the meetings later that day thinking the best of him and hopefully making a lasting impression on him. My friend wanted to control his reputation with this person and, therefore, any other person that person might come into contact with. We all have a propensity for trying to control, and often even over-control, how we are viewed or thought of by others.

"Rank me with whom thou wilt" means that we are giving up our pursuit to be known or identified for anything in particular, good or bad. To pray, "rank me with whom thou wilt," is to place ourselves before God to be used by God for God's purposes, regardless of the conclusions that people make about us, either explicitly or implicitly impacting our reputation.

Our reputation should matter to us, of course. A good reputation reflects good character in most cases. There are times when people fool us, and we are surprised by the truth or by their true selves. We've all been surprised to learn that someone isn't who we think they are. However, in most cases, as we identify the character of others, we associate a reputation with them, whether good or bad. Therefore, it should matter to each one of us what others think about us—to the degree that our reputation is built on our life mirroring Jesus's life and not built on a certain platform or a favorable position in society.

Our reputation, however, shouldn't keep us from doing what's right. This is what the Wesley Covenant Prayer is getting at. When we humbly offer ourselves to be ranked with anyone, we open ourselves up for ridicule, judgment, dislike, disapproval, and insignificance. This is why we often say no to the impression the Holy Spirit leaves on our minds and hearts, because many times the word or deed the Holy Spirit is directing us to say or take on is in direct conflict with the beliefs or opinions that we want people to have about us.

> ## *Jesus ... did what was right, not what was best for his reputation.*

Jesus, a friend of sinners, did what was right, not what was best for his reputation. This is what "rank me with whom thou wilt" means—we do what is right, regardless of the labels put on us or the categories in which people place us. To be friends with tax collectors and sinners, as Jesus was, is to let your character and what is right guide your steps of action, regardless of how you will be seen by others. Irrespective of the opinions people may form about you or the beliefs they may develop about you or the rung in society in which they place you, to be ranked with whomever is to live in pursuit of mirroring the life of Jesus. This will, without a doubt, make you a conduit of God's mission and likely a question mark in the minds of onlookers.

Personal Reflection

- How important (or overly important) is my reputation to me?
- What do I want to be known for? Is what I want to be known for aligned with God's mission?

Group Discussion

- What does "rank me with whom thou wilt" mean to you?
- What does character have to do with a good or bad reputation?
- Share a story in which you felt the nudge of the Holy Spirit.
- How willing are you to be a question mark in the minds of others because of the company you keep or how others have "ranked" you?
- What would you say is the main idea of this part of the prayer?

Today's Challenge:

FEELING GUTSY?

Ask a coworker, relative, or friend (someone who knows you quite well) to describe your reputation—the story others tell about you. Ask them to write it out and text it or email it to you so you have it to reflect on.

Departing Prayer

God, as your Son modeled what it means to be a friend of sinners, we pray that we would be known as a friend of sinners. Regardless of our reputation or the rung on society's ladder on which we are placed by others, give us the strength, courage, and commitment to do your work as you see fit. Amen.

DAY SIX

"PUT ME TO DOING,"

Today's Scripture Reading

After these things, the Lord commissioned seventy-two others and sent them on ahead in pairs to every city and place he was about to go. He said to them, "The harvest is bigger than you can imagine, but there are few workers. Therefore, plead with the Lord of the harvest to send out workers for his harvest. Go! Be warned, though, that I'm sending you out as lambs among wolves. Carry no wallet, no bag, and no sandals. Don't even greet anyone along the way. Whenever you enter a house, first say, 'May peace be on this house.' If anyone there shares God's peace, then your peace will rest on that person. If not, your blessing will return to you. Remain in this house, eating and drinking whatever they set before you, for workers deserve their pay. Don't move from house to house. Whenever you enter a city and its people welcome you, eat what they set before you. Heal the sick who are there, and say to them, 'God's kingdom has come upon you.' Whenever you enter a city and the people don't welcome you, go out into the streets and say, 'As a complaint against you, we brush off the dust of your city that has collected on our feet. But know this: God's kingdom has come to you.'"

Luke 10:1-11

Reflection

In order to understand the short four-word phase in the prayer, "Put me to doing," we have to understand it within the context of the second part of the phrase, another simple four-word phrase, "put me to suffering." The suffering, which we will discuss in the next daily reflection, can be interpreted as what happens when we take on the life that Jesus lived—a life of mission and ministry that will cost us something and require that we die to self-interests and take on the interests of Jesus.

If "Put me to doing" in Jesus's name is best understood as knowing that the work God gives us is the kind of work that Jesus would do, we might even say, "Give me the kind of work in which I will likely suffer." That raises the next question, "What is the kind of work that Jesus did in which he clearly suffered?"

The kind of work Jesus did is really quite simple. As you know, simple and easy are not always synonyms, so there is nothing easy about doing the kind of work in the world today that Jesus did when he walked about Israel teaching, healing, caring for, and rebuking. Yes, of course Jesus suffered on the cross. Jesus's humiliating death on the cross is where he suffered most. However, Jesus also suffered in many other ways. Again, we'll dig deeper into Jesus's suffering in the next daily reflection. The point is that to pray, "Put me to doing," is intricately linked to "put me to suffering."

Our work today, to reflect the suffering work of Jesus, is similar work. It is a multifaceted work marked by two types, or maybe better said, marked by two sides of a coin—work *for* the people on one side and work *with* the people on the other side.

> *We are to be images of God's love, and our prophetic message is in how we articulate God's saving grace in our lives.*

Work *for* the people was Jesus as he took on a prophetic ministry in which he brought the message of God to the people, as the Word of God or the *logos*. Of course, we do not confuse ourselves with ever being the *logos*—God Incarnate. We do, however, in a prayer of "Put me to doing," recognize that we are here on earth to represent God to all those we come into contact with. We are to be images of God's love, and our prophetic message is in how we articulate God's saving grace in our lives. The gospel message is simple. The gospel message is that in Jesus Christ, there is salvation and justice. When we are "put to doing," we are placed before people to share the good news, the gospel. This side of the coin is the evangelical gospel that transforms the souls of the very people Jesus came to seek and to save—the people searching for purpose and meaning, and for hope.

A deeply committed disciple recognizes that work *for* the people means that we are the storytellers of God's amazing grace. In Acts chapter 1, Jesus instructed his disciples to stay in Jerusalem, after forty days of teaching them about the kingdom of God, and he told them to wait for the Holy Spirit. The disciples, although they had no idea to that point what Pentecost would look like, were previously briefed on who the Holy Spirit was. They knew who the Holy Spirit was because of, among other ways, the teaching Jesus gave them in what we refer to as the Upper Room Discourse, which can be found in John 14–16.

Jesus told them in Acts 1:8 that the power of the Holy Spirit would be given to them. It would come upon them and, out of that power, they'd be the witnesses to the life of Jesus. Jesus was essentially saying that the way people would now come into contact with Jesus would be through their work and witness, word and deed.

We are now the ones giving evidence of Jesus's true redeeming work. The same Holy Spirit that came upon the disciples in Jerusalem and sent them out to save thousands sends us out into the world to bear witness to God's redeeming work. We are "put to doing" God's work when we advocate for people by sharing God's amazing good news that in Jesus Christ, there is salvation and justice.

Working *with* the people is priestly work. This is the social side of the coin. One side of the coin is the evangelical side, as noted above, and the other side of the coin is the social gospel. A social gospel demands we right the wrongs of the world and in doing so, apply Christian ethics to everyday problems. We right the wrongs for all people, especially for the vulnerable and oppressed—those who face such issues as economic inequality, poverty, racism, educational opportunities or lack thereof, environmental concerns, gender inequality, slavery, and many other forms of subjugation. The work of Jesus was to meet the everyday needs of the poor, the sick, and the burdened of any kind, and to tackle the systemic issues of injustice.

To pray, "Put me to doing," then, is to open our minds, hearts, and hands to carry out God's mission to restore the world toward its intended wholeness by practicing what Jesus practiced— sharing the good news and restoring society— in order to reveal the reign of God. Just as the disciples were sent to preach the good news and heal the world around them, so are we sent to do the work of God in the world. This work is both *for* the people and *with* the people. It is soul work, so to speak, and it is social justice.

Personal Reflection

- Have I ever served in such a way that it has cost me something?
- How willing am I to suffer like Jesus did to do God's work?

Group Discussion

- How did Jesus suffer in his earthly work?
- What is the difference between work *for* people and the work *with* people?
- Describe your understanding of the gospel.
- Do you agree with the author's description of the gospel? Why or why not?
- What are the top three social concerns facing the people you know?
- What would you say is the main idea of this part of the prayer?

Departing Prayer

Open our minds, hearts, and hands to bear witness to your work in this world, in both word and deed. Amen.

Today's Challenge:

TWO CONCEPTS, ONE COIN

There are two sides to the gospel coin: the evangelical side and the social gospel side. Today, carry a coin in your pocket. Throughout the day, take it out and hold it in the palm of your hand. As you hold it, pray that God would give you one opportunity to share your faith and one opportunity to meet the need of a person you come into contact with.

DAY SEVEN

"...PUT ME TO SUFFERING."

Today's Scripture Reading

So the king gave the order, and they brought Daniel and hurled him into the pit of lions.

The king said to Daniel: "Your God—the one you serve so consistently—will rescue you."

A single stone was brought and placed over the entrance to the pit. The king sealed it with his own ring and with those of his princes so that Daniel's situation couldn't be changed. The king then went home to his palace and fasted through the night. No pleasures were brought to him, and he couldn't sleep. At dawn, at the first sign of light, the king rose and rushed to the lions' pit.

As he approached it, he called out to Daniel, worried: "Daniel, servant of the living God! Was your God—the one you serve so consistently—able to rescue you from the lions?"

Then Daniel answered the king: "Long live the king! My God sent his messenger, who shut the lions' mouths. They haven't touched me because I was judged innocent before my God. I haven't done anything wrong to you either, Your Majesty."

The king was thrilled. He commanded that Daniel be brought up out of the pit, and Daniel was lifted out. Not a scratch was found on him, because he trusted in his God. The king then ordered that the men who had accused Daniel be brought and thrown into the lions' pit—including their wives and children. They hadn't even reached the bottom of the pit before the lions overpowered them, crushing all their bones.

Daniel 6:16-24

Reflection

Who in their right mind would want to be put to suffering? Deeply committed disciples, that's who. Deeply committed Christians realize that there is something bigger than their own self-interests, now and always, at work in the world. Deeply committed disciples know that this bigger work, or more specifically stated, the mission of God, is more important than their personal well-being, comfort, security, and social status.

I'm reminded of the account in Luke 9 when Jesus was walking along the road and someone said to him, "I will follow you wherever you go" (Luke 9:57). Clearly, as a way to show support for Jesus and his authority, this person shouted something they didn't mean. As the story continues, Jesus tells the person, "Foxes have dens and the birds in the sky have nests, but the Human One [Jesus] has no place to lay his head" (9:58). Jesus tells another person to follow him, and that person says, "Let me go and bury my father" (9:59), which is another way of saying something like, "It's going to be a while, Jesus; my dad isn't dead yet and, therefore, I haven't gotten my inheritance. I can't take on a life on the move, one of pilgrims, until my family affairs are in order."

Clearly, one of the lessons of this passage is that regardless of the physical, emotional, spiritual, and financial hardships we may face or the customs and conveniences of life we wish to have, we are to be "put to suffering." Deeply committed Christians voluntarily relinquish their rights and privileges. Simply stated, genuine followers of Jesus are to (1) die to self-interests and concerns, (2) yield wholeheartedly to God's plan, and (3) resist the desires of this world.

In Matthew 6:24 ("No one can serve two masters. Either you will hate the one and love the other, or you will be loyal to the one and have contempt for the other. You cannot serve God and wealth"; see also Luke 16:13), Jesus teaches that a person cannot have two masters. One will be loved and one will be hated, or one will attract our loyalty while the other is ignored. Jesus teaches that God and wealth cannot both be served. I believe that the wealth Jesus is talking about in these passages extends well beyond what we might consider wealth or personal possessions today.

I believe that if Jesus showed up in our churches to teach today, Jesus could very well spend his time teaching about God and wealth and serving the two, but also that you cannot serve *any* interest that distracts from serving God—more than wealth, in other words.

In a similar way, God instructs the Israelites, as one of the Ten Commandments, that "You must have no other gods before me," and "Do not make an idol for yourself," and "Do not bow down to them or worship them" (Exodus 20:3-5). Jesus is teaching in the above verses that you can only have one God and serve one God. Suffering for God's sake means we avoid having idols and other gods.

> ## Suffering for God's sake means we avoid having idols and other gods.

To die to our self-interests, yield to God's plan, and resist the desires of this world mean that we avoid keeping idols and gods, like a family inheritance that keeps us from following Jesus. We have all kinds of purging that needs to take place when we think about and speak of idols and gods. Work, our careers, chasing success, accumulating possessions, cultivating our personal image, sexual pleasures, or anything of the like that intoxicates us and consumes us might all be considered idols. "Put me to suffering" doesn't mean you can't have any of those things. It does, however, mean that they should not be allowed to creep in and take a place of priority in your life. We suffer when we push past what we want and live into what God wants for our lives.

"Put me to suffering," therefore, is to join Jesus in his deliberate life choices to suffer (or bear, or endure). This means we assume the loss of what we think we are entitled to and eligible for—our idols and gods—and audaciously pursue a simple life in the way of Jesus. A life in the way of Jesus is marked by profound behaviors of love, peace, hope, forgiveness, compassion, mercy, and other traits that continue endlessly.

"Put me to suffering" is to increase both the frequency and duration of the holy moments in our lives and in doing so, completely surrender to the mission of God, regardless how "beneath us" the work might be. PhD, MD, or CEO might mean we are needed to exercise our expertise, specialized skills, education, and vast experience. It may also mean that we might need to give up our titles and trophies and simply meet the practical needs of everyday people in everyday ways—needs like acceptance, encouragement, affirmation, affection, and appreciation at the most basic levels.

To pray, "put me to suffering," is to pray, "God, above all else and with all obedience, I place your will first in my life."

Today's Challenge:
SUFFER FOR JESUS

Name three ways that you can suffer for Jesus today. Pick one of the three ways you have listed and do it. Describe to another person what it felt like to be "put to suffering."

Personal Reflection

- Do I really believe that God's mission is more important than my own well-being, comfort, security, and social status?
- Do I tell God (and others) that I will follow Jesus wherever he goes, when I don't really mean my words?

Group Discussion

- What does it mean to die to self?
- What does it mean to yield wholeheartedly?
- What does it mean to resist personal desires?
- Describe a time when you served in a situation that others might consider was beneath you.
- What would you say is the main idea of this part of the prayer?

Departing Prayer

Teach us, God, to give up our titles and trophies and make meeting the needs of the people we know and come into contact with the number-one priority in our lives. Amen.

PART TWO

HONOR AND HUMILITY

PART TWO

HONOR AND HUMILITY

The first part of the Wesley Covenant Prayer impresses upon us the importance of surrendering and suffering. In the second part of the prayer—as I have ordered the prayer, anyway—we are presented with another set of striking themes: honor and humility.

It is possible that the original intention of this part of the Wesley Covenant Prayer was a challenge to stretch our perspective away from surrendering ourselves and toward participation in God's mission. We are to do this even with the possibility and likelihood that it may lead to some kind of suffering, and move us toward embracing the apparent contradiction between honor and humility. As a result of taking part in God's mission to restore the world toward its intended wholeness, we are honored, or we are humbled. This recognition reminds us, as deeply committed disciples, that we are to surrender ourselves to God for God's use, regardless of any potential outcome.

To be honored is to be held in high regard or great esteem. It is to be given praise for our actions and accomplishments. This part of the prayer guides us toward a posture of knowing that we may be honored for our participation in God's mission. However, it is very likely that we will also be humbled.

To be humbled is to be brought low. The word *humble* actually comes from the Latin *humilis* and literally means "low." When we carry out

God's work in the world, we might be honored. We might also, conversely, be humbled and be seen as someone who is commonplace and of little importance or significance.

Of course, when we embrace this humility and accept the position we obtain because of it, either in perception or actuality, we experience the absence of pride. The absence of pride is authentic humility. Humility is one of the essential virtues of human condition, along with other virtues, such as temperance, chastity, and charity. When embraced, authentic humility is a sign of holiness. It is a sign of purity of the heart. Pride most often involves competition. Humility is devoid of competition. Humility levels the playing field, so to speak, so that we are nothing more or nothing less than the people around us.

As we move our way through the second part of the Wesley Covenant Prayer, look for ways the prayer sheds light on the key themes of honor and humility. Deeply committed disciples learn to live in meekness, whether being honored or humbled. The key lesson in this particular part of the prayer is about being highly respected or made low. Either way, it is God's work, not ours.

DAY EIGHT

"LET ME BE EMPLOYED BY THEE OR LAID ASIDE FOR THEE,"

Today's Scripture Reading

Therefore, if you were raised with Christ, look for the things that are above where Christ is sitting at God's right side. Think about the things above and not things on earth. You died, and your life is hidden with Christ in God. When Christ, who is your life, is revealed, then you also will be revealed with him in glory.

So put to death the parts of your life that belong to the earth, such as sexual immorality, moral corruption, lust, evil desire, and greed (which is idolatry). The wrath of God is coming upon disobedient people because of these things. You used to live this way, when you were alive to these things. But now set aside these things, such as anger, rage, malice, slander, and obscene language. Don't lie to each other. Take off the old human nature with its practices and put on the new nature, which is renewed in knowledge by conforming to the image of the one who created it. In this image there is neither Greek nor Jew, circumcised nor uncircumcised, barbarian, Scythian, slave nor free, but Christ is all things and in all people.

Therefore, as God's choice, holy and loved, put on compassion, kindness, humility, gentleness, and patience. Be tolerant with each other and, if someone has a complaint against anyone, forgive each other. As the Lord forgave you, so also forgive each other. And over all these things put on love, which is the perfect bond of unity. The peace of Christ must control your hearts—a peace into which you were called in one body. And be thankful people. The word of Christ must live in you richly.

Teach and warn each other with all wisdom by singing psalms, hymns, and spiritual songs. Sing to God with gratitude in your hearts. Whatever you do, whether in speech or action, do it all in the name of the Lord Jesus and give thanks to God the Father through him.

Colossians 3:1-17

Reflection

We want to feel useful to others. We want to feel productive. We want to know that our talents, skills, gifts, and strengths are being used to their fullest, so we can continue working and contribute positively to the mission of God. It's really quite simple—human beings were created to work, subdue, rule, serve, and keep.

Genesis 1:26 says, "Then God said, 'Let us make humanity in our image to resemble us so that they may take charge of the fish of the sea, the birds in the sky, the livestock, all the earth, and all the crawling things on earth.'" You'll notice the words *take charge*, as they illuminate the fact that we are created to subdue and rule. Genesis 2:15 says, "The LORD God took the human and settled him in the garden of Eden to farm it and to take care of it." In this verse, you'll notice that God settles human beings in the garden for two reasons: "to farm it" and "to take care of it." When God was establishing the foundations of life on earth, God directed humans to be productive by partnering with God to take care of the earth. Long before Genesis 3, when humans make the selfish decision to try and snatch God's authority, God presents a mission opportunity for humans to partner with God to keep the earth whole.

In Genesis 1–2, God passes on to human beings the authority and responsibility to care for creation. We don't possess the authority; we hold it—like a parent who gives the keys to the car to the teenager for a quick trip to the store. The teen holds the keys for a while, but the keys, along with the car, belong to the parent. The role of the teen is to take the responsibility seriously and to steward the owner's possession. This passing on of God's authority to care for creation is not a license to impose our own will on it or abuse or misuse the land in some way, but to make sure that creation thrives.

Because of this meaningful task of stewarding God's creation, our hands are to remain active. We've been directed to diligently take charge of, farm, and take care of God's good and beautiful creation. This is why humans feel the need to be productive—we've been designed to work. This is also why, in part, God instituted the Sabbath, to take our hands off the work and to rest, remembering who and what sustains us—God.

"Let me be employed by thee" is a way of praying, "I want to be active for you, God. I want to use my talents, skills, gifts, and strengths to be productive in accomplishing your work." To be employed by God is to be engaged, eventful, and used by God for God's good work in the world. Praying this part of the prayer is a way of letting God know we want to be productive for God's purposes.

> *To be employed by God is to be engaged, eventful, and used by God for God's good work in the world.*

The opposite of being employed is being laid aside or unemployed. This is a much harder part of the prayer to pray. To be laid aside is to be idle and fruitless. I know of no one who wishes to be laid aside. However, I know of many who, for various reasons, are unable to be as productive as they wish they could be. Chronic pain, depression, disability, and aging are all factors that play into the reality that all of us become, at some point in our lives, less productive.

A few days ago, I received an email from someone I used to work with. This person shared that due to a decline in sales, his business was no longer able to keep him employed. He was reaching out to me for networking purposes, wondering if I knew anyone who was hiring. He described leaving on good terms, with a deep respect for the owners of the business who, for well over a decade, had kept every promise they had ever made to him, including monthly paychecks, reimbursement of business expenses, commissions on going above and beyond sales quotas,

Today's Challenge:

CREATION CARE

Take a walk outside in nature and make a list of three observations of God's creation. Listen for sounds, smell a flower, watch water flow, or pick a leaf off the ground and observe its intricacies. If the weather permits you to be outside, you can be productive by picking up trash and discarding properly.

and end-of-the-year bonuses. In his email, my friend wrote, "The more generous the owners were, the more I loved them. The more I loved them, the harder I worked. The harder I worked, the more results. The more results, the more generous the owners were. It was a wonderful partnership...and now, it is all gone."

This is tough stuff. As I write, the COVID-19 pandemic is wreaking havoc on every aspect of life. The emotional, financial, physical, relational, spiritual, and social aspects of everyday life have been upended. The unemployment rate in the United States is somewhere in the double digits and rising. People are being "laid aside" left and right, and our country looks more like it did in the Great Depression era than it does the swelling economic position of a few short months ago.

My friend, like so many other people I know, is reeling and trying to figure out what is next. After over a decade, he is finding his way again and having a very difficult time. He said, "The hardest part, Chris, is that I worked so hard for so long now that I have no idea what to do with myself. I am bored out of my mind. I feel so useless and so inadequate."

To pray, "or laid aside for thee," could very well mean we are waiting for what is next in our lives and while doing so, like my friend, we feel useless and inadequate. We likely could struggle to find meaningful activity—the kind of activity in which we find purpose and feel like we are positively contributing to something bigger than ourselves. Being "laid aside" for God can very well be a form of suffering, of being made low.

To pray, "or laid aside for thee," is recognition of at least three things. First, it is God's good work in the world, and we get to participate in it. Second, our gifts aren't merely for our own good; they are for the good of the world and, therefore, we are employed at God's discretion to accomplish God's work. Finally, to pray, "or laid aside for thee," is a humble recognition that regardless of active or idle, productive or unproductive, God determines the path of our labors. In doing so, God originates our position as employed or laid aside. In the end, to pray, "Let me be employed by thee or laid aside for thee," is a commitment to honor God, regardless of the conditions and circumstances of our life.

Personal Reflection

- Does my desire to be productive get in the way of following Jesus?
- In what ways am I intentional about caring for God's creation?

Group Discussion

- Do you practice a Sabbath time each week? Describe your Sabbath practice.
- What does it mean to you to be "employed" for God?
- Describe a time when you felt "laid aside."
- How do you feel about the idea of our gifts not being for us?
- What would you say is the main idea of this part of the prayer?

Departing Prayer

As we use our hands to serve you, God, remind us that we were made to take care of creation and to use our unique gifts, talents, and strengths to serve your purpose in this world. If we are laid aside, help us to wait patiently and expectantly. Amen.

DAY NINE

"...EXALTED FOR THEE OR BROUGHT LOW FOR THEE."

Today's Scripture Reading

So, a person should think about us this way—as servants of Christ and managers of God's secrets. In this kind of situation, what is expected of a manager is that they prove to be faithful. I couldn't care less if I'm judged by you or by any human court; I don't even judge myself. I'm not aware of anything against me, but that doesn't make me innocent, because the Lord is the one who judges me. So don't judge anything before the right time—wait until the Lord comes. He will bring things that are hidden in the dark to light, and he will make people's motivations public. Then there will be recognition for each person from God.

Brothers and sisters, I have applied these things to myself and Apollos for your benefit. I've done this so that you can learn what it means not to go beyond what has been written and so none of you will become arrogant by supporting one of us against the other. Who says that you are better than anyone else? What do you have that you didn't receive? And if you received it, then why are you bragging as if you didn't receive it? You've been filled already! You've become rich already! You rule like kings without us! I wish you did rule so that we could be kings with you! I suppose that God has shown that we apostles are at the end of the line. We are like prisoners sentenced to death, because we have become a spectacle in the world, both to angels and to humans. We are fools for Christ, but you are wise through Christ! We are weak, but you are strong! You are honored, but we are dishonored! Up to this very moment we are hungry, thirsty, wearing rags, abused, and homeless. We work hard with our own hands. When we are insulted, we respond with a blessing; when we are harassed, we put up with it; when our reputation is attacked, we are encouraging. We have become the scum of the earth, the waste that runs off everything, up to the present time.

1 Corinthians 4:1-13

Reflection

Humans thrive on having certain emotional needs met. Some of the emotional needs we look for are encouragement, acceptance, appreciation, affection, and to be comforted. In addition to these important needs, we also long for recognition. We like to be acknowledged for our efforts. We like to be given credit for the work we've done. We like others to greet the work we have done—such things as finding a solution, developing a new process, fixing something that is broken, inventing something new, creating a masterpiece—with praise and tributes. Some of the most dignifying and satisfying words we can hear are, "Good job" or "Well done."

As a result of this need, many of us strive for awards like employee of the month or top-performing salesperson or teacher of the year or most valuable player. There is nothing wrong, of course, with striving for these accolades—as long as chasing these honors and acknowledgments doesn't consume us. As long as the competition doesn't move us further from Christlikeness, it can actually be a healthy pursuit to succeed.

> *Striving for greatness and excellence is fine, but not at the expense of others.*

I don't know about you, but several times in my life, I've unhealthily chosen to pursue accolades and, therefore, gotten offtrack in my spiritual life. My passion and pursuit for prizes, so to speak, has overridden my compassion and connection to people. This has resulted in hurt relationships, an overinflated ego, or unhealthy practices in which I neglected eating right and sleeping well and counted successes over

Today's Challenge:

SECRET SERVICE

Find a way to serve someone today without the person knowing about it. Ideas may include writing a note, mowing the lawn or shoveling the snow, sending flowers or a plant, dropping a small gift on the person's doorstep, and so forth.

serving others. Again, striving for greatness and excellence is fine, but not at the expense of others I've trampled over to achieve it.

To be brought low is to be humbled. We don't typically chase this, since to be made humble or brought low can mean humiliation, feelings of indignity, or even embarrassment. To pray, "brought low for thee," means regardless of what the outcome our participation in God's good work might generate, we voluntarily accept it, knowing that we are God's vessels willing to take on a lowly position in the minds of others.

Have you ever worked your backside off on a project only to have no one recognize the work you've put in? Have you ever thought to yourself, *I know they'll recognize my work this time*, only to have no one even mention the work? This can happen in doing God's work too. It is very possible that in doing God's good work that no one single person will recognize what you are doing. God might be honored, but others might even seem disinterested. This truth is a very real possibility when we partner with God's mission.

"Exalted for thee or brought low for thee" prayed authentically means that we will accept any position, whether it be high or low, in order to be used by God. Acknowledgment or not, we open our minds, hearts, and hands to God's work and willingly assume recognition and respect or possible disregard and disdain.

When we pray the Wesley Covenant Prayer, we do so with the condition that, regardless of the outcome, we still commit to being actively or inactively employed or laid aside for God. Deeply committed disciples don't choose roles based on possible outcomes; we simply say yes to God. Deeply committed disciples know that there is tremendous worth found in the process of doing and what we learn from the process. Deeply committed disciples also know that doing God's work and completing assignments

God gives us is its own unique prize. If outside fulfilment is the objective that drives us, we are doing it for the wrong reason.

Personal Reflection

- What emotional needs do I have that need to be met? Am I faithfully meeting the emotional needs of others?
- Do I long to be recognized or exalted? Am I okay to be brought low?

Group Discussion

- How important are accolades to you? Has there ever been a time in your life when they consumed you?
- Describe a time when you've been "brought low" or humbled by God's work.
- What do you think it means to be God's vessel?
- What would you say is the main idea of this part of the prayer?

Departing Prayer

Regardless of being exalted or brought low, train us to say yes to your work. Also, train us to accept any position, high or low, for the sake of the world. Amen.

DAY TEN

"LET ME BE FULL,"

Today's Scripture Reading

The LORD is my shepherd.
  I lack nothing.
He lets me rest in grassy meadows;
  he leads me to restful waters;
    he keeps me alive.
He guides me in proper paths
  for the sake of his good name.

Even when I walk through the darkest valley,
  I fear no danger because you are with me.
Your rod and your staff—
  they protect me.

You set a table for me
  right in front of my enemies.
You bathe my head in oil;
  my cup is so full it spills over!
Yes, goodness and faithful love
  will pursue me all the days of my life,
  and I will live in the LORD's house
  as long as I live.

Psalm 23

Reflection

To be full is to be fulfilled or satisfied. There will be times in our accomplishing of God's work that we will feel contented and pleased, like when our thirst for meaning and purpose is quenched. To pray, "Let me be full," is like saying, "Let me feel happy and pleased with my contribution to your work, God."

There are times when we feel like we were specifically designed for the work we are doing or that the work was assigned expressly with us in mind. In this regard, God's work of mission and ministry hardly feels like a job—it actually brings us life. We are exuberant and joyful when we feel full, and this feeling of being full compels us to find more and similar types of ministry opportunities that will satisfy our longing to feel like we are making a difference.

The times that I feel full are when I have the chance to use my spiritual gifts to contribute to God's work. Most notably, I feel full when I have the privilege to teach small or large groups of people. A few years ago, I was asked to speak at a one-day church retreat. I took a late-night Friday flight out of Kansas City so that I could arrive by early Saturday morning to drive from the airport to the church. The church was two hours from the airport. The day of the retreat was the same day as a Notre Dame football game—the first game of the season. The church was less than ten miles from Notre Dame's campus in South Bend, Indiana. You know where this is going! I was told there would be about one hundred people there, but less than two dozen showed up. The pastor who invited me apologized profusely. Sure, I would have loved to have had one hundred people there. However, at the end of the day, when I sat back down on the plane on the way home, I felt so filled up. Teaching, training, keynote talks, and other opportunities to speak all help me feel full, regardless of how many people are in the room.

I also feel full when I coach others and see improvements made. For the last ten years, I have coached kids and teenagers in baseball. I feel full when I have the chance to lead a project from start to finish—the harder it is, the more I feel full. I feel full when a person I share my faith with joins me at church and takes a step closer to following Jesus. I feel full when I finish a manuscript and turn it in to the publisher. You get the picture, I am sure. We feel full when we live into the jobs and responsibilities we do well.

We are full when purpose and meaning align. A sense of purpose helps us to feel the work we were made to do is useful and beneficial. Meaning, embedded within purpose, provides us with a sense of knowing the value or worth we bring to the purpose. In the words of the great writer Frederick Buechner, "The place God calls you to is the place where your deep gladness and the world's deep hunger meet."* This is where purpose and meaning converge. If purpose is where we find "gladness" and meaning is where the world's "hunger" is met, then we are where we are meant to be. Where we are meant to be leaves us with a feeling of satisfaction and completeness, or the feeling of being "full."

> *"The place God calls you to is the place where your deep gladness and the world's deep hunger meet." –Frederick Buechner*

Outside influences can make us feel full too. For example, the friendships we have, the goals we accomplish, the growth we experience, the community we know and love, and the stories of transformation we tell can all contribute to being satisfied or full.

"Let me be full," as we will see in the next reading, is only one fragment of this part of the prayer. Just as "to be employed" has a counterpart—"to be laid aside"—"full" also has its opposite, "empty." However, today we are exploring what it means to be full. Let's finish our reflection today with the encouragement that when we are full, let's be sure to be grateful to God and say, "Thank you." Let us never take our fullness for granted. We should also be intentional about reminding ourselves to thank others, express appreciation through sharing credit with others, and noting achievements—both big and small. Paying attention to these important aspects of gratitude will train us to overcome potential feelings of smugness and entitlement, and allow us to experience the abundance of joy.

Personal Reflection

- How often do I feel happy or content?
- What brings me the most joy in life? What fuels my desire to serve more?

---

* Frederick Buechner, *Wishful Thinking: A Seeker's ABC* (HarperOne, 1993), 119.

Group Discussion

- Where did your deep gladness and the world's deep hunger overlap?
- Describe a time when you felt "full" from doing God's work.
- In what ways are you intentional about being grateful and saying "thank you" to God?
- What would you say is the main idea of this part of the prayer?

Today's Challenge:

OVERLAP

Take ten minutes today to fill in the illustration at the bottom of this page. Reflect on the question in the center.

Departing Prayer

God, give us moments in which we feel full from doing your work. Guide us to take time to reflect on what makes us feel full and then to celebrate the moments in which we experience it. Finally, train us to be grateful in all times, especially when we experience the happiness and satisfaction of participating in your mission. Amen.

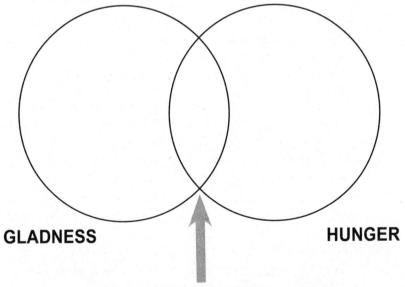

GLADNESS   **HUNGER**

WHAT DOES THIS FEEL LIKE?

DAY ELEVEN

"...LET ME BE EMPTY."

Today's Scripture Reading

So then, with endurance, let's also run the race that is laid out in front of us, since we have such a great cloud of witnesses surrounding us. Let's throw off any extra baggage, get rid of the sin that trips us up, and fix our eyes on Jesus, faith's pioneer and perfecter. He endured the cross, ignoring the shame, for the sake of the joy that was laid out in front of him, and sat down at the right side of God's throne.

Think about the one who endured such opposition from sinners so that you won't be discouraged and you won't give up. In your struggle against sin, you haven't resisted yet to the point of shedding blood, and you have forgotten the encouragement that addresses you as sons and daughters:

> *My child, don't make light of the Lord's discipline*
> *or give up when you are corrected by him,*
> *because the Lord disciplines whomever he loves,*
> *and he punishes every son or daughter whom he accepts.*

Bear hardship for the sake of discipline. God is treating you like sons and daughters! What child isn't disciplined by his or her father? But if you don't experience discipline, which happens to all children, then you are illegitimate and not real sons and daughters. What's more, we had human parents who disciplined us, and we respected them for it. How much more should we submit to the Father of spirits and live? Our human parents disciplined us for a little while, as it seemed best to them, but God does it for our benefit so that we can share his holiness. No discipline is fun while it lasts, but it seems painful at the time. Later, however, it yields the peaceful fruit of righteousness for those who have been trained by it.

Hebrews 12:1-11

Reflection

If to be "full" is to be satisfied, then to be "empty" is to be unfulfilled and void of any kind of satisfaction. To pray the second half of this line, "let me be empty," is to offer ourselves up knowing that there may be times when we serve God's mission that we are left wanting—feeling like our work is done in vain, without any real impact or joy. We've all heard statements similar to, "We all have parts of our jobs we don't like," or "I like 80 percent of my job and hate 20 percent of my job." In God's economy, however, there is likely a time or two when we will feel the 80/20 principle in reverse, or maybe even feel 100 percent dissatisfied.

To serve others, knowing that "empty" might be there to greet us at the end of our work, is to serve faithfully, without needing to see or feel the fruits of our labor. Empty can mean a lot of things, including lack of purpose or meaning. Contrary to being "full," serving empty can feel as though serving is pointless. To pray, "let me be empty," however, is to know that serving could be an experience in which we serve out of obedience and responsibility and never see positive results, meet joy, feel fulfilled, or make a difference of any kind.

A saying often attributed to Mother Teresa goes, "Don't think that love, in order to be genuine, has to be extraordinary." The truth is, sometimes loving others in the name of Jesus doesn't even feel ordinary. We must choose to love, even when we don't feel like it. We must choose to love, even when it doesn't produce feelings of satisfaction. Also attributed to Mother Teresa are the words, "For love to be real, it must cost, it must hurt, it must empty us of self." I believe that Wesley would have thought similarly. To love, that is to have a total love of God and others, we must be emptied of self. Like Jesus emptied himself to take on humanity (Philippians 2), so are we charged to take up our cross and in doing so, die to self and empty ourselves in entirety, which, of course, includes feelings of satisfaction.

I am sure you've been empty before. Empty is that feeling when you feel as though whatever you've done to serve or love another has had no impact, carries no weight, gets no credit, and takes every ounce of your energy to complete. In the end, you choose to love anyway because you know that this is how the world will recognize its disciples, by how we love one another—and by how we choose to live an illumined life in a dark world. You won't always feel joy, but you will always know the weight of the responsibility to love.

> ## *You won't always feel joy, but you will always know the weight of the responsibility to love.*

C. S. Lewis said, "The rule for all of us is perfectly simple. Do not waste time bothering whether you 'love' your neighbor; act as if you did."* Although we may feel empty, if we act as though we feel joy, those we serve will know that God has not forgotten them. Love enacted is a gift from God, whether we feel like giving it away or not.

Have you ever received a gift that you didn't really like? What did you say? You said, "Thanks so much; I love it," even when you didn't. Have you ever been proudly served a meal by someone who has spent a great deal of time working on it and after taking one bite, you realized you were going to have to choke it down? What did you say? You said, "This is delicious; thank you." You may have even gone overboard and said, "May I have the recipe for this?" I would assume you've also told a person their painting or drawing or clay pot was beautiful, when really you were thinking, *That's awful.* Here is the reality when we pretend to like something we don't, only we know we are pretending. Unless, of course, we are bad actors. Regardless of the possibility of feeling empty, we pretend we are full anyway and, in doing so, we show love. Playacting love is a not a departure from reality, but rather a journey into the center of it.

---

* . C. S. Lewis, *Mere Christianity* (Macmillan: New York, 1952), 116.

Personal Reflection

- How often do I feel empty?
- Am I willing to remain empty for God's work? For how long am I willing to feel empty?

Group Discussion

- When have you served and felt empty?
- What do you think emptying ourselves has to do with serving?
- Describe a time when you loved, even when you didn't feel like it. How did you feel after you loved?
- What would you say is the main idea of this part of the prayer?

Today's Challenge:
ORDINARY LOVE

Make a list of five ordinary ways to love. After you act on the ordinary ways, rate your level of love during each action on a scale of 1 to 5, with 5 being full of love and 1 being left empty. Take note of what feelings you have and why.

Departing Prayer

May we, when feeling empty from loving others, call upon you, God, for strength to endure. May we love well, whether we feel like it or not. Amen.

DAY TWELVE

"LET ME HAVE ALL THINGS,"

Today's Scripture Reading

Now if you really obey the LORD your God's voice, by carefully keeping all his commandments that I am giving you right now, then the LORD your God will set you high above all nations on earth. All these blessings will come upon you and find you if you obey the LORD your God's voice: You will be blessed in the city and blessed in the field. Your own fertility, your soil's produce, and your livestock's offspring—the young of both cattle and flocks—will be blessed. Your basket and your kneading bowl will be blessed. You will be blessed when you are out and about and blessed when you come back. The LORD will defeat any enemies who attack you. They will come against you from one direction but will run for their lives away from you in seven different directions. The LORD will command the blessing to be with you—in your barns and on all the work you do—and he will bless you on the land the LORD your God is giving you. The LORD will establish you as his own, a holy nation, just as he swore to you, if you keep the LORD your God's commandments and walk in his ways. All the earth's peoples will see that you are called by the LORD's name, and they will be in awe of you. The LORD will make good things abound for you—whether the fertility of your womb, your livestock's offspring, or your fertile soil's produce—on the very land that the LORD swore to your ancestors to give to you. The LORD will open up for you his own well-stocked storehouse, the heavens, providing your land with rain at just the right time and blessing all your work. You will lend to many nations, but you won't have any need to borrow. The LORD will make you the head of things, not the tail; you will be at the top of things, not the bottom, as long as you obey the LORD your God's commandments that I'm commanding you right now, by carefully doing them. Don't deviate even a bit from any of these words that I'm commanding you right now by following other gods and serving them.

Deuteronomy 28:1-14

Reflection

Here, it appears that the prayer shifts from an internal focus (being "full" or "empty") toward an external focus ("all things" or "nothing"). There are at least two ways to interpret the phrase, "Let me have all things." First, it could mean wants and wishes. Wants and wishes are the unnecessary but far too often welcomed "things" that give the craving person the luxuries and conveniences of life, the "extras," so to speak.

Extras are what many people associate with happiness and pleasure, only to find out that once the extras are attained, they don't fill that God-shaped void in our souls. This first interpretation, however, doesn't seem to fit Wesley's theology and perspective on the Christian life. I can't imagine that when Wesley prayed this prayer and led covenant prayer services he would have had in mind the idea that somehow God cared about his fortunes—well-being, perhaps, but not any possessions.

I have a very wealthy friend. When I say, "very wealthy," I mean crazy rich. Not quite Gates, Musk, or Bezos money, but more money than I can ever imagine what to do with. About ten years or so ago, this friend of mine engineered a piece of software that changed the landscape of how computer programmers and video game designers code or write software. A very large technology company purchased this for hundreds of millions of dollars. After many large purchases of glamourous homes, exotic cars and boats, and jewelry over the last ten years, he recently told me, "I thought I would be fulfilled by all these things I have bought. But, honestly, Chris, possessing all this stuff doesn't mean a thing to me anymore."

I specifically remember one day in which my friend drove his latest purchase, a very rare car that I think he has driven less than a dozen times, to my house to show it to me. As we stared at it, he said, "Yeah, I am blessed." I said, "You think God cares about this car? You aren't blessed because you own a car that less than one hundred people in the world have. You are blessed because you've been given life." The point is simply this: "All things" mean nothing if they aren't kept in proper perspective.

The truth is, some people are afforded the extras. Our human condition leads us to compare at times. We look around and ask questions like, "Why is it that so-and-so gets this, that, or the other, and we are left without?" Extras are just that—the unnecessary bonuses in life that might be fun to have and might bring moments of pleasure. In the end, however, the extras tend to disappoint us as they eventually become faded, dull, and monotonous.

Second, one could interpret the phrase, "Let me have all things," to mean something akin to "Let me have enough." I would contend that this is more of what Wesley had in mind. Enough is essentially abundance reframed and held in proper perspective. For many, enough is all they need. Then, what really matters comes into focus and we begin to see more clearly that "stuff" doesn't matter. What matters is our faithful commitment to seek God's idea of the good life, which is a life patterned after the mission, ministry, and message of Jesus.

> **What matters is our faithful commitment to seek God's idea of the good life, which is a life patterned after the mission, ministry, and message of Jesus.**

I realize that "all things" is the complement to "nothing," which we will explore in tomorrow's reading. I also realize that "all things" is one extreme end of the spectrum. Today, I want to suggest that one way to pray this prayer and find the middle of the spectrum is to pray that we might learn to live with enough. People who can learn to live with enough can learn to live honestly in the intent of the Wesley Covenant Prayer by choosing to live with a reframed perspective of "all things."

I have struggled to learn to live with an "enough" mentality. Often, if I am honest, I work in a sliding scale of what is "enough" to my struggles. The scale typically slides to accommodate my human instincts to collect and to own, mainly for feelings of control and security. I have learned a few tips to help me practice Jesus's teaching in Matthew 6:25-34. Before I share my tips, let's look at the Scripture passage first:

> "Therefore, I say to you, don't worry about your life, what you'll eat or what you'll drink, or about your body, what you'll wear. Isn't life more than food and the body more than clothes? Look at the birds in the sky. They don't sow seed or harvest grain or gather crops into barns. Yet your heavenly Father feeds them. Aren't you worth much more than they are? Who among you by worrying can add a single moment to your life? And why do you worry about clothes? Notice how the lilies in the field grow. They don't wear themselves out with work, and they don't spin cloth. But I say to you that even Solomon in all of his splendor wasn't dressed like one of these. If God dresses grass in the field so beautifully, even though it's alive today and tomorrow it's thrown into the furnace, won't God do much more for you, you people of weak faith? Therefore, don't worry and say, 'What are we going to eat?' or 'What are we going to drink?' or 'What are we going to wear?' Gentiles long for all these things. Your heavenly Father knows that you need them. Instead, desire first and foremost God's kingdom and God's righteousness, and all these things will be given to you as well. Therefore, stop worrying about tomorrow, because tomorrow will worry about itself. Each day has enough trouble of its own."

The simple conclusion is that each day has plenty of trouble on its own. Stop living with a scarcity mentality and trust God that you will have what you need. Here are three tips I have learned that have helped me to trust God more deeply every day to provide for me and my family:

1. **Learn to say no to items I don't truly need.** Since I turned eighteen, I have worked full time. Most of the years that have gone by since turning eighteen I have worked a full-time job and held a second part-time job too. I can't remember when I haven't had a full-time job and what I call a second street. My

main street is my job at Church of the Resurrection; my second street is writing this book. Because of my second streets over the years, I have never really had to say no. If I have wanted it, and I thought I would use it, I'd buy it. Over the last few years, however, in order to give more, I have decided I would say no to the items that I (or my family) don't really need. This has allowed me to give more money away and to learn what enough really means.

2. **Make people the priority, not pleasures or possessions.** When the people around you—family, strangers, coworkers, neighbors, friends, clients—become the priority and serving their needs becomes a consistent discipline in our lives, pleasures and possessions seem almost immediately inconsequential. Taking action on others' urgent or even semi-urgent needs begets a spirit of generosity. A spirit of generosity begets hope, and hope, of course, is the prevailing confident expectation that in God's economy, there is enough for everyone.

3. **Save to give over save to live.** As I have learned how to say no and worked, with failure and flaws, of course, to make people the priority, I have seen that saving money for the purpose of giving to those individuals and organizations in need is fun. My family and I have a blast deciding who we can help and then helping them. Our commitment to simply living with enough gives my wife and three kids a way to rally and work on a project together. Last month, at the suggestion of my youngest son, who is fifteen, we fed fifteen individual families for five days each. Instead of saving to live with more, we've been saving to give more, and honestly, it is so much fun!

Deeply committed disciples discipline themselves to avoid falling into the trap of chasing "stuff" and by being consumed by the wants and wishes of life. Instead, deeply committed disciples choose simplicity—they choose to be content with enough. "Let me have all things" is not a prayer for resources and reserves. Within the context of the whole prayer, these short words guide deeply committed disciples toward surrender and humility, especially when the "all things" counterpart of "nothing" is a very real possibility.

Personal Reflection

- Do I struggle with "things"?
- With what do I associate happiness?

Group Discussion

- Do you ever find yourself comparing your "stuff" with that of others? In what ways?
- Do you ever find yourself comparing your happiness to others? In what ways?
- What do you think it means to have enough?
- How do you avoid falling into the trap of chasing stuff?
- What would you say is the main idea of this part of the prayer?

Today's Challenge:

THE GIVEAWAY

Pick an item of yours that has value or that you associate value to. Select a person to give it to, and then give it to them.

Departing Prayer

Help us to see with eyes of compassion and not eyes of comparison. Teach us, God, to learn to be content with enough and avoid the chasing of material possessions. Also, where we see those without enough, grant us the ability to help. Amen.

DAY THIRTEEN

"...LET ME HAVE NOTHING."

Today's Scripture Reading

One day Job's sons and daughters were eating and drinking wine in their oldest brother's house. A messenger came to Job and said: "The oxen were plowing, and the donkeys were grazing nearby when the Sabeans took them and killed the young men with swords. I alone escaped to tell you."

While this messenger was speaking, another arrived and said: "A raging fire fell from the sky and burned up the sheep and devoured the young men. I alone escaped to tell you."

While this messenger was speaking, another arrived and said: "Chaldeans set up three companies, raided the camels and took them, killing the young men with swords. I alone escaped to tell you."

While this messenger was speaking, another arrived and said: "Your sons and your daughters were eating and drinking wine in their oldest brother's house, when a strong wind came from the desert and struck the four corners of the house. It fell upon the young people, and they died. I alone escaped to tell you."

Job arose, tore his clothes, shaved his head, fell to the ground, and worshipped. He said: "Naked I came from my mother's womb; naked I will return there. The LORD has given; the LORD has taken; bless the LORD's name." In all this, Job didn't sin or blame God.

Job 1:13-22

Reflection

The opposite side of having "all things" is having "nothing." Continuing onward in the Wesley Covenant Prayer, we remain rooted within the concept of an external focus of our life. Whereas feeling "full" or feeling "empty" are internal areas of focus, "all things" and "nothing" are areas of external focus. Focusing on external matters guides us to the realization that by professing to God, self, and others that it will be okay with us if, as a result of our yielding to God's will in this covenant prayer, we end up with "nothing."

Most of us have no idea what it is like to have nothing. Most of us don't even know someone personally who actually knows what it is like to have nothing. Most of us, consequently, read or say this part of the prayer having no idea what we think we are giving ourselves up for. Are we really okay with having "nothing"? I grew up the son of a very hardworking pastor who mostly served rural churches. My mom worked equally as hard. She was an administrative assistant and a very good one at that, so her former employers tell me. We didn't have much growing up, but we had enough. My parents made sure that we had what we needed for school, extracurricular activities, athletics, and entertainment. We lived a very middle, middle-class life. I've never known what it is to have nothing.

> *Are we really okay with having "nothing"?*

I've befriended homeless people over the years who possess only what they can carry. I've known families who have lost everything in house fires, but were able to rebuild. I've heard stories and know a few individuals who have lost their businesses and would claim that they "lost everything." They, too, however, were able to rebuild and, in some cases, make a comeback, acquiring far more wealth than they had previous to the failed business. I struggle to recall the names of anyone I've met or known who I could truly say has nothing. My point? My point is simply this. Most of us, when we say these words in the Covenant Prayer, have no idea what they truly mean, and if we did, I think we'd be hesitant to speak it loudly or perhaps we might even be tempted to mumble the words or even skip them.

To pray, "let me have nothing," is to pray something similar to, "Take it all away." We've already started with something. For instance, you are reading this book and you are holding it in your hands—either in paperback, tablet, or device format; you are in possession of this book. If you possess this book, you have something, which is not nothing. That realization alone is what makes this part of the prayer so complex and difficult. So very few of us are actually aware of what it means to have nothing, or next to nothing, for that matter.

Personal belongings, meaningful relationships, fortunate circumstances, healthcare plans, bank accounts, shelter, love—the list of possessions can go on and on. Not only do most of us know what having these commonly understood life necessities feels like, we know what occupying them affords us—control and security. These necessities allow us to retreat and take refuge in our comfortable and safe domains in which we typically have sole control when the going gets tough. To pray, "let me have nothing," is effectively to pray, "I give up control and the so-called right to be secure."

I've been called a control freak. I like to have the reins, the helm, the wheel, the handlebars, whatever the best-suited metaphor is. I prefer to have the ability to control what is happening around me. Most of us, if we are honest with ourselves and others, feel the same way. It is hard to give up control. I still struggle with giving up control of my own life. This struggle results in a tendency for me to want to keep people distant. It can also mean, and has meant on many occasions, that I struggle to trust others completely.

Being a control freak can have its advantages. There have been times in my working life when someone needed to take charge. My desire to be in control has served me well in these types of situations. Most of the time, however, my desire to be in control causes me to want to have the last word, makes me painfully slow in accepting when I am wrong, and can make me want to change others for my own benefit or the benefit of the project.

Over time, I have gotten better at letting go of the smaller things, recognizing fears that cause me to want to be in control, and expecting that not everything will go my way and there will undoubtedly be surprises of some kind that emerge. I've learned that taking the time to listen to the views, opinions, or ideas of others also helps me loosen my controlling grip. I've also learned that this need for control can become an obsessive need that keeps me from listening intently for the Holy Spirit's still, small voice and acting upon the nudges and impressions the Holy Spirit gives me. Control freaks have a very hard time praying, "Let me have nothing."

When Wesley prayed this portion of the Covenant Prayer and guided others to pray it with him in the Covenant Services he would lead, in my mind, he was essentially praying, "Regardless of any and all results, implications, or consequences of my promise to serve you, I will seek to do your will above all else." Honestly, we can't really pray one phrase of this particular aspect of this prayer and be truthful to the prayer. This is simply due to the fact that the vast spectrum of "all things" or "nothing" is what the prayer is essentially getting at. However, what if the phrase, "Let me have all things," was not in the prayer and we only had "let me have nothing" to pray? Would we still pray the prayer with such confidence and gusto? Would we pray to have "nothing" if having "all things" wasn't also an option?

Today's Challenge:
DRIVE, SERVE, OR WATCH

Choose one of the following three options.

1. Drive to a place in your city or town where it is assumed that people have "nothing."
2. Volunteer at a place where the people are assumed to have "nothing." Ideas include a rescue mission, soup kitchen, or homeless shelter.
3. Watch a documentary on homelessness or poverty.

After you have accepted and acted on one of the options above, reflect on your experience. Journal or share your thoughts with others as a way to make them memorable.

Personal Reflection

- Am I prepared to have nothing?
- How attached am I to the things I have?

Group Discussion

- Have you ever had, or felt like you had, nothing? Please explain.
- Have you ever been guilty of retreating to comfortable and safe situations? If so, can you provide an example?
- Do you serve with results or outcomes in mind? How might you change this?
- Would you pray this prayer if having nothing was guaranteed? Why or why not?
- What would you say is the main idea of this part of the prayer?

Departing Prayer

Lord, help us become less about control and more about conforming—conforming to your will. Let us also become people who are willing to have nothing for the sake of the world. Be honored by our commitment to your will and work. Amen.

DAY FOURTEEN

"I FREELY AND HEARTILY YIELD ALL THINGS TO THY PLEASURE AND DISPOSAL."

Today's Scripture Reading

Hear what the LORD is saying:
Arise, lay out the lawsuit before the mountains;
    let the hills hear your voice!
Hear, mountains, the lawsuit of the LORD!
        Hear, eternal foundations of the earth!
The LORD has a lawsuit against his people;
    with Israel he will argue.
"My people, what did I ever do to you?
        How have I wearied you? Answer me!
I brought you up out of the land of Egypt;
        I redeemed you from the house of slavery.
        I sent Moses, Aaron, and Miriam before you.
My people, remember what Moab's King Balak had planned,
        and how Balaam, Beor's son, answered him!
        Remember everything from Shittim to Gilgal,
            that you might learn to recognize the righteous acts
            of the LORD!"

With what should I approach the LORD
        and bow down before God on high?
Should I come before him with entirely burned offerings,
        with year-old calves?

Will the Lord be pleased with thousands of rams,
      with many torrents of oil?
Should I give my oldest child for my crime;
      the fruit of my body for the sin of my spirit?
He has told you, human one, what is good and
      what the Lord requires from you:
           to do justice, embrace faithful love, and walk humbly with
           your God.

Micah 6:1-8

Reflection

Whether we are full and have all things or we are empty and have nothing, to pray, "I freely and heartily yield all things to thy pleasure and disposal" is simply to encapsulate the possibility of the previous statements in the prayer. The previous two phrases confess that, regardless of the outcomes of our participation in God's mission, we generously and wholeheartedly, with an open hand and enthusiastic spirit, submit to God's will.

When we submit to God's will we are yielding to God's mission, which I have stated throughout this book is to restore the world toward its intended wholeness. God's will, then, is that creation would be made whole "on earth as it is in heaven." God's way of fulfilling the mission of the whole world is Jesus Christ. Jesus is the way (and the truth and the life) to wholeness. God's work in the world is agented and delivered by the church, you and me, faithfully abandoning our own desires and self-interest for the sake of the world, in the name of the Father, Son, and Holy Spirit.

"I freely and heartily yield all things to thy pleasure and disposal" is, in a sense, the capstone commitment we make indicating that we know full well, as deeply committed disciples, that God's desires and preferences trump any desires or preferences that we might have. We also know and make it obvious in this portion of the prayer that our participation in God's work likely will not be thrown away or disposed of, but, if it were, we'd be okay with that.

A couple years ago, I, along with most of my confirmation group— about fourteen thirteen-year-olds—volunteered at a nonprofit ministry center in Kansas City. This particular place stored household goods and furniture for people who were coming out of prison or addicts in recovery. Upon our group's arrival, we were greeted by a lovely woman who had been volunteering there three days a week for nearly ten years. Amazing, I know. Aside from this woman's story, the day was very unorganized. We made the best of it, however, and when we were told that the ministry needed us to organize the goods on the third floor, our group resolutely set out to make a dent in what was at first glance an overwhelming amount of work. I was glad I had fourteen young, strong, and energetic kids to rely on.

We worked eight hours solid, with a short break for lunch and various moments to goof off (like thirteen-year-olds do, and the forty-somethings who volunteered to lead them). We organized the third floor with thoughtfulness, putting couches with couches, recliners with recliners, rugs with rugs, box springs with box springs, and the list goes on and on. After a day's work, we were proud of our efforts and truly felt like we helped make it easier for people in need to see what was available to choose from.

Several of my confirmation students were unable to attend that day because of a basketball game. So, since serving was a mandatory aspect of completing confirmation, I took three of the boys from my group back the next weekend. Wouldn't you know, we were sent to the third floor. I said to the woman—the same woman who was there to welcome us the previous weekend—"Third floor, you sure?" She said, "Yes. Last weekend, another group came in and made a total mess of it! It needs to be organized." With what I am sure was a puzzled voice, I said, "Sounds good. We are on it," and off we went to the third floor, where I had spent eight hours apparently working for no reason. They considered all our efforts to have amounted to no more than a "complete mess." To my shock, the third floor was arranged completely differently. Eight hours of hard work was disposed of, tossed aside like it wasn't even helpful. The next day, a Sunday, our confirmation group met as usual and I told the group what had happened. One of the students spoke up and said, "It doesn't matter, Chris; we didn't do it so that people would think we did a good job. We did it to serve the best way we could, and that's what we did."

In addition to recognizing that our work can be disposed of and tossed to the side, we recognize that God is God and we are not. It is God's mission, not our mission. We, the church, are the created, chosen, blessed, commissioned, supported, and sent ones, agenting God's love in and to the world. We are not, however, the architects of the mission. Said differently, the Church does not have a mission; the mission has a Church. Therefore, God's authority exceeds all, and we are to know it, believe it, and live it.

> ## *The Church does not have a mission; the mission has a Church.*

A disciplined life, marked by submission, simplicity, and abandonment of our own interests, can guide us toward becoming cheerful givers instead of entitled consumers. Cheerful givers are generous with their entire lives. They give without expecting anything in return, and this is what God calls us to and what Wesley's prayer reminds us of. God undoubtedly uses us, and God has great plans for us to carry out God's mission in the world. The work we do in this mission we do cheerfully, knowing we are making a difference and participating with a plan much bigger than any one of us. However, even if God were to discard our work, we'd still do the work—cheerfully. This is what it means to "freely and heartily yield all things," and to do so, "for God's (thy) pleasure or disposal."

Personal Reflection

- Am I conscious of when I choose to yield to God's will and work?
- In what ways am I currently fulfilling God's mission?

Group Discussion

- In what ways do you struggle to yield wholeheartedly?

- Are there one or two struggles that are the hardest? If so, which ones?
- Would you say you are a cheerful giver? Why or why not?
- What would you say is the main idea of this part of the prayer?

Departing Prayer

Help us, God, to lead a disciplined life, marked by submission and simplicity. Also, God, may our lives be marked by abandonment of our own interests and measured by our faithful generosity toward others. Amen.

Today's Challenge:
RIGHT OF WAY

As you are out and about today, seek to find an opportunity for someone to get in line in front of you. Perhaps you'll be at a grocery store, a restaurant, the bank, in line for a ticket at the stadium, or in line at a coffee shop. Use this as a moment and a reminder of what it means to yield wholeheartedly.

PART THREE

COMMUNITY AND COMMITMENT

PART THREE

COMMUNITY AND COMMITMENT

The first part of this prayer impresses upon us the importance of surrendering and suffering. Part two presents us with the themes of honor and humility. Finally, in this third part of the prayer, we are offered two more captivating themes—community and commitment.

Community and commitment are essential ideas to the Wesley Covenant Prayer as they each take on more than mere words. Community and commitment take deeply committed disciples on a pilgrimage toward a new kind of covenant. This new kind of covenant is one in which we turn over our own interests and causes and choose to take on God's mission, which is to restore the world toward its intended wholeness.

Community, in a very broad view, is the sense we have of fellowship and friendship. Fellowship and friendship are the result of sharing common mindsets, interests, purposes, and ambitions. The product of aligning ourselves with those with whom we share important matters in common is a group of interdependent people who choose to share life together.

Authentically sharing life together narrows the understanding of community toward its finer attributes and qualities. Sharing life together is an intimate undertaking in which, among other fundamentals, love, trust, respect, honesty, attention, and ongoing two-way communication are required. These traits and qualities help us feel at home. Feeling at home means that we have found a person or a group of people to whom we can belong. A place where we belong is a place of forbearance and forgiveness, in which God is shaping us into who God desires us to be.

The third part of the Wesley Covenant Prayer turns our attention to community. It also turns our attention to commitment. Commitment is dedication, loyalty, and faithfulness. Like community, commitment isn't merely an idea; it is actually a state of being, a reality. All of us like the idea of commitment, but living in such a dynamic state can be difficult for us to maintain. The Wesley Covenant Prayer challenges our commitment to commitment, so to speak; it challenges our sustained faithfulness to God's mission.

Our commitment, in the end, is a direct result of how we understand community. For those we love, we choose devotion and loyalty. For those with whom we share a common purpose, we choose faithfulness. It can be said that the degree of our commitment is directly proportional to the depth of the community we experience. We commit to *who* matters, and we commit to *what* matters. The final third of this prayer is meant to help us establish *who* matters and *what* matters in our lives.

DAY FIFTEEN

"AND NOW, O GLORIOUS AND BLESSED GOD,"

Today's Scripture Reading

Who has measured the waters in the palm of a hand
    or gauged the heavens with a ruler
    or scooped the earth's dust up in a measuring cup
    or weighed the mountains on a scale
    and the hills in a balance?
Who directed the LORD's spirit
    and acted as God's advisor?
Whom did he consult for enlightenment?
    Who taught him the path of justice and knowledge
    and explained to him the way of understanding?
Look, the nations are like a drop in a bucket,
    and valued as dust on a scale.
    Look, God weighs the islands like fine dust.
Lebanon doesn't have enough fuel;
    its animals aren't enough for an entirely burned offering.
All the nations are like nothing before God.
    They are viewed as less than nothing and emptiness.

So to whom will you equate God;
    to what likeness will you compare him?
An idol? A craftsman pours it,
    a metalworker covers it with gold,
    and fashions silver chains.
The one who sets up an image chooses wood that won't rot
    and then seeks a skilled artisan
    to set up an idol that won't move.
Don't you know? Haven't you heard?
    Wasn't it announced to you from the beginning?

Haven't you understood since the earth was founded?
God inhabits the earth's horizon—
>   its inhabitants are like locusts—
>   stretches out the skies like a curtain
>   and spreads it out like a tent for dwelling.
>   God makes dignitaries useless
>   and the earth's judges into nothing.
Scarcely are they planted, scarcely sown,
>   scarcely is their shoot rooted in the earth
>   when God breathes on them, and they dry up;
>   the windstorm carries them off like straw.
So to whom will you compare me,
>   and who is my equal? says the holy one.

Isaiah 40:12-25

Reflection

We are moving into the final part of the prayer. In doing so, we are shifting our attention *away from* ourselves—as we have laid claim to who we want to become—and *to* who we claim God is. We claim, of course, to be people who are willing to surrender and suffer, people who desire to honor God over self and even to being humbled. We also claim that we are people who are willing to do God's great work in the world recklessly or wastefully, meaning without any care for outcome or result. We have told God through prayer that even if God were to dispose of our work, we'd still do it.

The words *And now* indicate turning toward a new idea or area of focus. Essentially, the words *And now* would be like saying, "Therefore." So, it isn't a stretch at all to think that what we are really saying when we say the words *And now* is something like, "With all that in mind" or "In summary of all that has been said" or "According to my previous declarations" or "Subsequent to all that I have expressed so far." This turning toward a new area of focus by saying, "And now," is meant to help us carry forward the preceding ideas, not turn away from them.

"O, glorious and blessed God" is a beautiful statement. It is a statement of designation. When we say, "O, glorious and blessed God," we assign supremacy to God, acknowledging God's reign and rule. We are also indicating our awareness that God is magnificent, full of wonder and mystery, unable to be truly fathomed, and worthy of celebration. We worship when we say, "O, glorious and blessed God." It isn't that we don't worship when we say the entire prayer—we certainly do, as prayer is a robust form of worship. With these words, however, we take a moment, a singular and distinctive moment, to revere God and recognize God's holiness and sacred divinity.

> *God is magnificent, full of wonder and mystery, unable to be truly fathomed, and worthy of celebration.*

If you've ever studied the attributes of God, you know how important they are to Christians and our understanding of God and of our faithful worship of God. A baseline belief in God's existence and trusting God's existence for life is the foundation for building a robust relationship with God. We do not become who God intends for us to be without an understanding of who God is and what God is like. Jesus gives us a clear and compelling picture of who God is. In the life, death, burial, resurrection, and ascension of Jesus (and all that takes place between those anchoring points), we see the express representation of God. For greater clarity, read these words from the writer of Hebrews:

> In the past, God spoke through the prophets to our ancestors in many times and many ways. In these final days, though, he spoke to us through a Son. God made his Son the heir of everything and created the world through him. The Son is the light of God's glory and the imprint of God's being. He maintains everything with his powerful message. After he carried out the cleansing of people from their sins, he sat down at the right side of the highest majesty. And the Son became so much greater than the other messengers, such as angels, that he received a more important title than theirs.
>
> Hebrews 1:1-4

Today's Challenge:

YOU ARE

Write a prayer to God. Include in the prayer at least five attributes of God (grace, mercy, compassion, omnipresence, and so forth). Avoid asking God for anything (petition), so that you can fix your eyes on God and God's majesty.

Jesus is the language of God. This means, according to Hebrews, specifically verse 2, that God's method for communicating who God is and what God is like to humans is the person of Jesus. God's dialect with God's creation is God Incarnate, Jesus.

We know what God is like from the Old Testament, as Hebrews says, "through the prophets to our ancestors," and we know God by means of what is called "general revelation." General revelation is God's way of revealing God to humans through the physical universe and through human reasoning—all natural means. "Special revelation" is also how we are to understand God. Special revelation is the means that God uses to reveal God to us—means such as the Bible, God's Word, and Jesus, God's Son. When we pray, "O glorious and blessed God," we are praying with the knowledge of God as God has chosen to reveal God to us.

There are, of course, many attributes of God. The four most commonly understood attributes of God among Christians, new and mature, are:

1. Omnibenevolence— God's ability to remain wholly loving to all for all times
2. Omnipresence— God's ability to be wholly present everywhere at all times
3. Omniscience— God's ability to be wholly aware of all things at all times
4. Omnipotence— God's ability to be wholly powerful over all things at all times

In summary, when we pray, "O, glorious and blessed God," we are hallowing God's name. Remember, "Our Father, who art in heaven, hallowed be thy name…"? This is what we are doing when we are declaring that we recognize all the attributes we associate with God in our thinking and our being. The truth of the matter is that we cannot pray all that we have previously prayed and not recognize God's supremacy and incomparability. To neglect or avoid this crucial part of the prayer would be to devalue the entire prayer. Sure, we could choose to say words other than *glorious* or *blessed* and still be true to the spirit of the prayer. The particular words we choose are not as important as the action of pausing and taking the singular and distinctive moment in time to worship the Almighty God.

To worship God is to return to God what is due to God by responding from the transparency of our heart. When we pray the Wesley Covenant Prayer, we worship, of course. When we pray, "O, glorious and blessed God," we reveal the symphony resonating in our hearts, minds, and souls.

Personal Reflection

- Do my claims and my behaviors match?
- When others tell the story of me, would they say that I am humble? Why or why not?

Group Discussion

- What are your three favorite attributes of God and why?
- How do you define *worship*?
- Fill in the blank: God, I am most grateful for _____.
- What would you say is the main idea of this part of the prayer?

Departing Prayer

God, you are majestic.
We praise your name.
We praise your holy name.
We praise your holy, all-powerful name.
We praise your holy, all-powerful, infinite name.
We praise your holy, all-powerful, infinite, ever-loving name.
Amen.

DAY SIXTEEN

"...FATHER, SON, AND HOLY SPIRIT,"

Today's Scripture Reading

At that time Jesus came from Galilee to the Jordan River so that John would baptize him. John tried to stop him and said, "I need to be baptized by you, yet you come to me?"

Jesus answered, "Allow me to be baptized now. This is necessary to fulfill all righteousness."

So John agreed to baptize Jesus. When Jesus was baptized, he immediately came up out of the water. Heaven was opened to him, and he saw the Spirit of God coming down like a dove and resting on him. A voice from heaven said, "This is my Son whom I dearly love; I find happiness in him."

Matthew 3:13-17

Reflection

Our singular moment of worship—not singular in the sense that it is the *only* moment of worship within the prayer, but rather singular in the sense that it is emphasized or brought out of the familiar and meant for astonishment—continues as we recognize all persons of the Trinity: Father, Son, and Holy Spirit. This phrase of the prayer builds upon the phrase, "And now, O, glorious and blessed God," which in one sense is a prelude to the grander announcement, "Father, Son, and Holy Spirit." Naming the Trinity is perhaps naming the biggest mystery of God in Christianity. To evoke the Trinity, then, in the form of prayer might very well be the most profound act a Christian can carry out.

There are numerous analogies for the Trinity. I am sure you've heard most of them. There is the egg (shell, white, yolk), water (ice, steam, liquid), the human being (body, soul, spirit), the propeller (three blades), and the cake (dry ingredients, wet ingredients, icing). All analogies fall short for a variety of reasons. They are, even though they are not perfect, helpful for trying to wrap our minds around the mystery. The most helpful of analogies is likely the three-leaf clover which, of course, consists of the stem and three leaves representing God (the stem) and Father, Son, and Holy Spirit (three leaves). This is the analogy said to have been used by St. Patrick to evangelize the Irish during the fifth century. Irrespective of the analogies, nothing can decisively frame an understanding of God.

The early Christians thought it important to develop and advance the doctrine of the Trinity. Our Apostles' Creed clearly describes three persons that are co-equal and co-eternal. The Father is the Almighty, Creator of all things. The Son is the image of the Father, our Lord and Savior. The Spirit is the extension of God in action, the power and breath of God. Although each of these persons of the Godhead is separate, the main point is that in them, there is unity. The Trinity is a picture of an authentic relationship—a personal, relational, loving connection.

Wesley undoubtedly desired that those who said the prayer along with him understand that the relationship between God and humans was stitched together by God's holy love. To name, "Father, Son, and Holy Spirit," is to declare that a relationship exists. Wesley was citing an intimacy with God that superseded all other aspects of human-only relationships, and that also identified the fullness of God in which relationships can exist and thrive.

> *To have a relationship with God means that we are stitched together by holy love.*

Today's Challenge:

PIECE OF CAKE

If you have time, bake a cake or cupcakes. As you bake, remember the Trinity is one God in three persons— Father, Son, and Holy Spirit, just as there are dry ingredients, wet ingredients, and icing. If you do not have time to bake, buy a cupcake or several to share with family and friends.

To have a relationship with God means that we are stitched together by holy love. This means that we are chosen, valued, and protected. To be **chosen** means that we are God's children (John 1:12), friends of Jesus (John 15:15), invited to live in communion with Jesus (1 Corinthians 6:17), complete in Jesus (Colossians 1:13-14), and have access to God through Jesus (Hebrews 4:14-16.) To be **valued** means that we have worth to God. God values us by giving us opportunity to host God as God's temple (1 Corinthians 3:16) and to be partners with God in God's mission as ministers of reconciliation (2 Corinthians 5:16-21). Finally, to be **protected** in our loving relationship with God means that we are citizens of heaven (Philippians 3:20), that we are anointed by God (2 Corinthians 1:21-22), and that we are given assurance that God is working in all things for our (those who love God) ultimate good (Romans 8:28).

When we pray, "Father, Son, and Holy Spirit," it is important to pray knowing that we have a real relationship with God (the Trinity) and not just an intellectual acknowledgment of a detached God who rules from a distant throne and loves with a withdrawn heart. Quite the opposite, in fact. God loves us and desires a closeness that comes from a desire for us to draw near to God and deepen our commitment to Christ.

In addition, when we pray, "Father, Son, and Holy Spirit," we also identify the missional nature of God revealed in Scripture. God the Father sends God the Son. God the Son sends God the Spirit. God the Spirit sends us, the Church, into the world. Wesley prayed this prayer to illuminate the fact that we, the Church, the people of God, are the agency that God is using to restore the world toward its intended wholeness. God is a missionary God who is worthy of our unbroken devotion and faithful effort to participate in God's mission. This is one of the most fundamental aspects of not only this particular part of the prayer, but the prayer in its entirety. This reality expands the prayer beyond a personal prayer and develops it into a communal prayer. When we pray the Wesley Covenant Prayer, we do so in communion with the Church and in solidarity with our fellow followers of Jesus.

Personal Reflection

- What is the biggest mystery of God to me?
- How would I explain the Trinity? What analogy would I use? Why?

Group Discussion

- What analogy of the Trinity do you find most helpful? Why?
- What words would you use to describe the fullness of God?
- What do you think it means that we are the agency that God is using to restore the world?
- In what ways is the Wesley Covenant Prayer communal?
- What would you say is the main idea of this part of the prayer?

Departing Prayer

Father, Son, and Holy Spirit, we love you deeply. We offer a confession for the things we have done and for the things we have left undone. We ask for your forgiveness. May we, with our attitude, behaviors, and lifestyle, honor you. We remember, God, that you are a relational God longing for our complete love. May we offer you our love with the way we worship you and treat others. Amen.

DAY SEVENTEEN

"...THOU ART MINE, AND I AM THINE."

Today's Scripture Reading

Dear friends, let's love each other, because love is from God, and everyone who loves is born from God and knows God. The person who doesn't love does not know God, because God is love. This is how the love of God is revealed to us: God has sent his only Son into the world so that we can live through him. This is love: it is not that we loved God but that he loved us and sent his Son as the sacrifice that deals with our sins.

Dear friends, if God loved us this way, we also ought to love each other. No one has ever seen God. If we love each other, God remains in us and his love is made perfect in us. This is how we know we remain in him and he remains in us, because he has given us a measure of his Spirit. We have seen and testify that the Father has sent the Son to be the savior of the world. If any of us confess that Jesus is God's Son, God remains in us and we remain in God. We have known and have believed the love that God has for us.

God is love, and those who remain in love remain in God and God remains in them. This is how love has been perfected in us, so that we can have confidence on the Judgment Day, because we are exactly the same as God is in this world. There is no fear in love, but perfect love drives out fear, because fear expects punishment. The person who is afraid has not been made perfect in love. We love because God first loved us. Those who say, "I love God" and hate their brothers or sisters are liars. After all, those who don't love their brothers or sisters whom they have seen can hardly love God whom they have not seen! This commandment we have from him: Those who claim to love God ought to love their brother and sister also.

1 John 4:7-21

Reflection

Relationship experts will tell you that what matters most for healthy, enduring relationships, particularly marriages and families, is a combination of factors, such as commitment, faithfulness, generosity, patience, forgiveness, trust, proximity and time, communication, and selflessness. The mutual connection two or more people share is dependent upon each person's willingness to graciously give to the other without expecting anything in return—this is community.

Community, from the Latin, *communitas*, literally means "with gifts." The individual members of couples, families, or small groups realize that all of who they are and all of what they have is meant for the sake of the others. When this notion becomes practical, or real, no one is in need. This, of course, is the story of the early church as we understand it from Acts, such as in chapter 2 and 4. Those particular passages describe a community in which "there were no needy persons among them" (Acts 4:34). Acts 2 and 4 give us a beautiful image of a loving community. Love is not only the impetus for such sharing and intimacy found within the communities of the very early church, it is also the outcome, producing a virtuous cycle in which to orient our lives.

Unlike the English language, which is limited to one word for love, the Greek language provides us with at least four words. These four words are *eros*, *storge*, *philia*, and *agape*. You've probably heard of these words. *Eros* is love on a physical level. *Storge* is love on or at the familial level. *Philia* is personal affection or love on a friendship level. *Agape*, however, is considered by many as a different kind of love, a different dimension of love altogether. Where *eros*, *storge*, and *philia* are natural ways to describe our emotional connection and heartfelt response to one another, *agape* love is more of a person's quality than it is a different kind of love.

> **Agape *love comes from God.***
> ***It is a perfect love.***

Agape love comes from God. It is a perfect love. In fact, we can only *agape* because God first *agape(d)* us. This fatherly love of God, the kind of love that drives out fear and makes us perfect, is on display in God's longing to be in relationship with humanity and to restore creation to wholeness. *Agape* love orders our lives, develops and defines our character, and yields a mutual connectedness to one another that drives our selfless actions toward others. First Corinthians 13:1-13 is likely the most well-remembered passage about love (along with John 3:16) that gives us a clear picture of what *agape* love is:

> If I speak in tongues of human beings and of angels but I don't have love, I'm a clanging gong or a clashing cymbal. If I have the gift of prophecy and I know all the mysteries and everything else, and if I have such complete faith that I can move mountains but I don't have love, I'm nothing. If I give away everything that I have and hand over my own body to feel good about what I've done but I don't have love, I receive no benefit whatsoever.

> Love is patient, love is kind, it isn't jealous, it doesn't brag, it isn't arrogant, it isn't rude, it doesn't seek its own advantage, it isn't irritable, it doesn't keep a record of complaints, it isn't happy with injustice, but it is happy with the truth. Love puts up with all things, trusts in all things, hopes for all things, endures all things.

> Love never fails. As for prophecies, they will be brought to an end. As for tongues, they will stop. As for knowledge, it will be brought to an end. We know in part and we prophesy in part; but when the perfect comes, what is partial will be brought to an end. When I was a child, I used to speak like a child, reason like a child, think like a child. But now that I have become a man, I've put an end to childish things. Now we see a reflection in a mirror; then we will see face-to-face. Now I know partially, but then I will know completely in the same way that I have been completely known. Now faith, hope, and love remain—these three things—and the greatest of these is love.

This particular part of the Wesley Covenant Prayer, "thou art mine, and I am thine," is deeply personal. While the prayer pertains to groups of all sizes, it is meant to establish the friendship between the pray-er and

God, individually. To pray, "thou art mine, and I am thine," is to honor and celebrate the affection that God has for us and that we have for God. Additionally, to pray this portion of the prayer is to admit reliance upon God for initiating the relationship, to highlight that it is God's *agape* love that shapes the pathway of our lives, as love is the dominant theme to the Christian ethic, and to esteem the truth that in God we are loved unconditionally and entirely. This truth creates an enduring mutuality.

Personal Reflection

- What matters most to me in my relationships?
- Where do I find community? What's my role in helping others find community?

Group Discussion

- What about experiencing community is most important to you?
- Why do you think *agape* love is considered more than a kind of love and a quality of a person?
- In what ways do you seek and find companionship with God?
- Do you agree that love is the central theme of the Christian life? Why or why not?

Today's Challenge:

REFLECT AND INVITE

Take a moment to reflect on the community in which you find a safe, secure, and welcoming place. As you identify the community(ies) where you belong, be sure to send a text, email, letter, or make a phone call to tell those in your community how much they mean to you and the impact they have in your life. Take the challenge to another level by seeking someone you know who is in need of community and invite the person to join yours.

Departing Prayer

May our lives be known for agape love—the kind of love that drives out fear and is complete. Order our lives accordingly. Make us the selfless people you desire us to become. In the name of your Son Jesus's name, we pray. Amen.

DAY EIGHTEEN

"SO BE IT."

Today's Scripture Reading

As soon as Solomon finished praying and making these requests to the LORD, he got up from before the LORD's altar, where he had been kneeling with his hands spread out to heaven. He stood up and blessed the whole Israelite assembly in a loud voice: "May the LORD be blessed! He has given rest to his people Israel just as he promised. He hasn't neglected any part of the good promise he made through his servant Moses. May the LORD our God be with us, just as he was with our ancestors. May he never leave us or abandon us. May he draw our hearts to him to walk in all his ways and observe his commands, his laws, and his judgments that he gave our ancestors. And may these words of mine that I have cried out before the LORD remain near to the LORD our God day and night so that he may do right by his servant and his people Israel for each day's need, and so that all the earth's peoples may know that the LORD is God. There is no other God! Now may you be committed to the LORD our God with all your heart by following his laws and observing his commands, just as you are doing right now."

1 Kings 8:54-61

Reflection

Quite honestly, "So be it" is a peculiar phrase. Some people use this phrase as a way of saying, "I do not agree with it, but I will accept it." Others translate this phrase to mean, "Since I can't change it, I'll live with it." Still others might interpret this phrase to mean something akin to resignation or surrender, a way of saying, "I give up. You win."

Wesley's intention of speaking this phrase, in my opinion, likely meant something altogether different. Wesley's use of "So be it" was an indication that he was not simply passively accepting the responsibilities identified and expressed in the prayer. Rather, Wesley was deliberately accepting the responsibilities and was going to be intentional about enthusiastically seeking ways to act. We might presume that Wesley was saying, "It is as I have prayed it. I understand it, and I accept it. Let it be true in me."

When we pray, "So be it," we are making a statement to God, in the same way Wesley did, that we are deliberately accepting the responsibilities and that we will enthusiastically seek ways to act. When I was in college, I joined the U.S. Navy Reserve. I did so for many reasons: to serve the people of our country, to help cover the costs of my education, to get a trade skill (heavy equipment operation) that I could fall back on in case the "pastor thing" didn't work out, and to join the long list of Navy veterans in my family. It was a fantastic experience. I learned so much about discipline, honor, leadership, loyalty, and a host of other important character qualities. Much of what I learned still serves me today as I lead teams, develop people, and complete projects.

> *When we pray, "So be it," we are making a statement to God...that we are deliberately accepting the responsibilities and that we will enthusiastically seek ways to act.*

I still vividly remember the day I stood at the MEPS (military entrance processing station) in upstate New York and took my Oath of Duty. After meeting the physical requirements and passing the aptitude tests, meeting with a Navy counselor to pick my job, and reviewing the military codes of conduct, I was placed in a room with other soon-to-be shipmates, and in front of the U.S. flag, a picture of the President, and the MEPS commanding officer. I raised my right hand and said, "I swear." "I, *Christopher W. Folmsbee*, do solemnly swear to support and defend the Constitution of the United States . . . obey the orders of the President of the United States . . . so help me God." After the Oath of Duty, I was bound to the terms of my contract and would be held accountable for my actions or inactions.

The words *So be it* remind me of my Oath-of-Duty experience. Essentially, I was telling the United States Department of Defense that I was accepting the responsibilities of my duty and that I was going to be intentional about enthusiastically seeking ways to act on the responsibilities. This is how I view my words *So be it* in the Wesley Covenant Prayer. I am declaring my willingness to serve God and God's mission to restore the world toward its intended wholeness.

This phrase, "So be it," is used in this portion of the prayer, much like the "Amen" at the end of the prayer—to condense the principles and precepts within the prayer and express sincere agreement with them. Wesley was not granting his approval of the principles and precepts. After all, they are not his to approve. Wesley was profoundly, albeit succinctly, conveying his acceptance to take on the challenge to embody the prayer. "So" means referring back to all that was previously mentioned. "Be" indicates that what exists is true. "It" refers to exactly what matters.

Let it be true in each of us that we accept the principles and precepts which are both implicit and explicit within the prayer. In doing so, we embody the person and work of Jesus, who modeled to all what it means to sacrifice so that the world might know and for the sake of others.

Personal Reflection

- How committed am I to the Wesley Covenant Prayer?
- How willing am I to pray, "Let it be true of me"?

Group Discussion

- How would you describe the phrase, "So be it"?
- So far, what are the most profound principles and precepts of the prayer to you? Why?
- In what ways can we embody the prayer every day where we live, work, study, or play?
- What would you say is the main idea of this part of the prayer?

Departing Prayer

Gracious God, we completely surrender all to you! You are worthy of all our praise. As we kneel in worship to you, feel our love, devotion, and loyalty. By the working power of the Holy Spirit, convict us and guide us to live in such a way that reveals our agreement with your truth. May you approve of our lives. Amen.

DAY NINETEEN

"AND THE COVENANT WHICH I HAVE MADE ON EARTH,"

Today's Scripture Reading

Now these are the commandments, the regulations, and the case laws that the LORD your God commanded me to teach you to follow in the land you are entering to possess, so that you will fear the LORD your God by keeping all his regulations and his commandments that I am commanding you—both you and your sons and daughters—all the days of your life and so that you will lengthen your life. Listen to them, Israel! Follow them carefully so that things will go well for you and so that you will continue to multiply exactly as the LORD, your ancestors' God, promised you, in a land full of milk and honey.

Israel, listen! Our God is the LORD! Only the LORD!

Love the LORD your God with all your heart, all your being, and all your strength. These words that I am commanding you today must always be on your minds. Recite them to your children. Talk about them when you are sitting around your house and when you are out and about, when you are lying down and when you are getting up. Tie them on your hand as a sign. They should be on your forehead as a symbol. Write them on your house's doorframes and on your city's gates.

Deuteronomy 6:1-9

Reflection

A bold reminder that this prayer is more than passing thoughts or fleeting words, Wesley makes a promise when he prays, "And the covenant which I have made on earth." More strongly stated than the word *promise*, we could essentially say that Wesley makes a contract. A contract is a formal spoken agreement, and using a word like contract (or pact, treaty, or accord) takes this prayer from something we might have an inclination to undervalue—as human promises hardly carry the weight they ought to—and assigns an unmistakable significance to the prayer.

The majority of phrases in the Wesley Covenant Prayer require that they be tied to either the preceding or succeeding statement to fully grasp the context and appreciate and comprehend the main idea. This particular phrase, to be held in context, must be understood as linked to the succeeding statement of "let it be ratified in heaven." While the covenant is made on earth, it requires God's blessing to be wholly authorized.

Wesley wishes to elevate his commitment, or take it up a notch, and makes a covenant to prove his words are more than mere lip service to surrender, suffering, humility, and the like. Unlike the covenants in Scripture, in which God outlines the roles and responsibilities and which there is no negotiation, Wesley makes a human attempt to raise the stakes of the prayer left undone. Wesley knows he will struggle to perfect the prayer. The practical reality is that there will be times he fails to do as his words say he will, and so is true for us. However, his desire is that he not fail and that he perfects the prayer by flawlessly living out the principles and precepts.

What is required of a Christian? What exactly are we saying yes to when we choose to follow Jesus? I realize that Wesley's covenant is in the context of the previous statements made in the prayer. Through the prayer, Wesley surrenders himself, even to the possibility of suffering, and commits to serve God in honor or in humility. Wesley also chooses to live in community with God and participate in God's missional commitment to restore the world. Wesley is naming the requirements for him (and others who wish to follow) to fully live into God's mission, beginning with the realization that he is no longer his own and continuing to the commitment that he is bound to the remarks he is making in the prayer. As Christians, without even any knowledge of the Wesley Covenant Prayer, what are we committing to when we become Christians? What are we contracting with God to do?

There are many ways to answer the question of the Christian

commitment. For me, the most basic way to answer the question, "What is required of a Christian?" is summed up in what we call the Great Commandment, to "love God and love others." When they say yes to following Jesus, Christians commit to strive to perfectly love God and perfectly love others. Jesus said, *"love the Lord your God with all your heart, with all your being, and with all your mind,"* and, *"You must love your neighbor as you love yourself"* (Matthew 22:37, 39; see also Mark 12:30-31 and Luke 10:27).

> **When they say yes to following Jesus, Christians commit to strive to perfectly love God and perfectly love others.**

To be faithful Christians, we must grow inwardly in our adoration of God and outwardly in our expression of love to others. This is what Christians say yes to. This is what it means, in part, to be a follower of Jesus. This inward growth means that we surrender to God, abide with God, and worship God with all of our lives, which begins on the inside, in the heart. The outward growth means that we live in such a way that speaks truth or bears witness to God's love. We seek to restore a community of people, reminding them that God has not forgotten them, and we impart life or give away our own interests and desires for the sake of the world, placing God's kingdom activity first. The inward and outward formation in our lives, loving God and loving others, happens in harmony. This means these two areas of formation are inseparable—you don't do one without the other. We can't choose which one we like better and then live by only that one. A virtuous life in the way of Jesus is about the identification of and, ultimately, the working out of both inward and outward formation, in chorus.

Now, back to the Wesley Covenant Prayer. Wesley isn't trying to usurp God's authority by originating the covenant. Instead, Wesley, by praying, "And the covenant which I have made on earth," is actually placing himself under the authority of God by inviting God to hold him accountable for his actions or inactions. This is a critical element of the prayer as Wesley, and all of us who pray with him, is opening up his heart as if to say, "Search me, know me, and discipline me, as I may stray."

Each of us is prone to wander, and Wesley knows this. Therefore, the covenant is a sincere act in which the desire to surrender to God's work is intensified. Deeply committed disciples know they wander, but the earnest desire of their heart is faithfulness that leads to perfect love.

Personal Reflection

- Do I keep my promises? Would others say I keep my promises?
- What is most significant to me about this part of the prayer?

Group Discussion

> **Today's Challenge:**
> # PROMISE-KEEPER TEST
>
> Ask a friend, relative, coworker, or neighbor (someone who knows you well) to answer this question:
>
> [Insert your name] keeps his or her promises:
>
> - all the time
> - some of the time
> - rarely
> - never

- Do you agree that covenants on earth require God's blessing to be authorized? Why or why not?
- What can we do, as a group, to hold one another accountable to the promises we make to God and others?
- Why do transparency and faithfulness matter?
- What would you say is the main idea of this part of the prayer?

Departing Prayer

Search us, O God, and know our hearts. Lead us in your everlasting and good ways. We submit ourselves to you as a living sacrifice, God, for your use and the use of your Kingdom. Let us no longer be conformed to this world, but be transformed that we may be a sacrifice to your perfect will. Amen.

DAY TWENTY

"...LET IT BE RATIFIED IN HEAVEN."

Today's Scripture Reading

The mountains may shift,
    and the hills may be shaken,
    but my faithful love won't shift from you,
    and my covenant of peace won't be shaken,
    says the LORD, the one who pities you.

Suffering one, storm-tossed, uncomforted,
    look, I am setting your gemstones in silvery metal
    and your foundations with sapphires.
I will make your towers of rubies,
    and your gates of beryl,
    and all your walls of precious jewels.
    All your children will be disciples of the LORD—
    I will make peace abound for your children.
You will be firmly founded in righteousness.
    You will stay far from oppression because you won't fear,
    far from terror because it won't come near you.
If anyone attacks you, it's none of my doing.
    Whoever attacks you will fall because of you.
Look, I myself created the metalworker who blows the fire of coal and
who produces a tool for his work.
    And I myself created the looter to destroy.
No weapon fashioned against you will succeed,
    and you may condemn every tongue that disputes with you.
This is the heritage of the LORD's servants,
    whose righteousness comes from me, says the LORD.

Isaiah 54:10-17

Reflection

As we have seen, the majority of the phrases in the Wesley Covenant Prayer necessitate that they be tied to either the preceding or succeeding statement in order to fully show the context and to identify the main idea. "Let it be ratified in heaven" is explicitly tied to its preceding phrase, "And the covenant which I have made on earth," and can't be isolated in its main idea, which is that, while the covenant is made on earth, it requires God's blessing to be wholly authorized.

God's blessing is simply God's approval or God's sanctification. This means, to pray, "let it be ratified in heaven," is to prayerfully seek God's satisfactory agreement that consists of mutuality and relevance. The Bible is full of places where people are soliciting God's blessing. The following show a number of places, just within the Psalms, in which God's blessing is pursued or mentioned:

> Because you, LORD, bless the righteous.
>   You cover them with favor [blessing] like a shield.
>   Psalm 5:12

> Yes, goodness [blessing] and faithful love
>   will pursue me all the days of my life,
>   and I will live in the LORD's house
>   as long as I live.
>   Psalm 23:6

> His anger lasts for only a second,
>   but his favor [blessing] lasts a lifetime.
> Weeping may stay all night,
>   but by morning, joy!
>   Psalm 30:5

> How great is the goodness [blessing]
>   that you've reserved for those who honor you,
>   that you commit to those who take refuge in you—
>   in the sight of everyone!
>   Psalm 31:19

> The LORD is a sun and shield;
>   God is favor [blessing] and glory.

The LORD gives—doesn't withhold!—good things
    to those who walk with integrity.
Psalm 84:11

    because you are the splendor of their strength.
By your favor [blessing] you make us strong
Psalm 89:17

Let the kindness [blessing] of the Lord our God be over us.
    Make the work of our hands last.
    Make the work of our hands last!
Psalm 90:17

When we pray, "let it be ratified in heaven," alongside Wesley—and countless other Christians past, present, and future—we are making certain to communicate that we know God is the one who sanctions any covenant that we might make, and we ask for God's blessing to make it so. We are one party in the contract, so to speak, and while our covenant might be genuine and sincere, it is only half of the needed equation in order for the treaty to be confirmed.

This understanding, of God being the confirmer of the covenant, is important for several reasons. First, it makes certain that we understand where authority dwells. We have a particular purpose and acquire meaning from our participation in God's mission, but it is God's mission and God reigns over our stated promises and God prompts our daily actions.

Second, praying, "let it be ratified in heaven," accounts for the supernatural and mysterious nature of God. God does the ratifying, but God does so from heaven—our future paradise. The kingdom of God is both already and not yet. This notion is a key linkage to the Wesley prayer as it takes into account that Jesus inaugurated the kingdom of God and that one day, the kingdom of God will be fully consummated. Consequently, the Kingdom is *already* here, but not all here *yet*. We await all things being made new, or whole, and while we wait, we do the redemptive work of God in the world through the power of the Holy Spirit so that earth looks like heaven.

Finally, when we pray, "let it be ratified in heaven," we do so realizing that God is not only the sending one who empowers us to do God's work, but also the one who evaluates the faithfulness with which we do the work.

Our work, while meant to be a witness to the world, is not evaluated by the ones around us; it is evaluated by God. Others may help us in our attempts to do the work by coming alongside of us for accountability, support, encouragement, and critique. Ultimately, though, God determines and measures the faithfulness in which we serve.

> *Our work, while meant to be a witness to the world, is not evaluated by the ones around us; it is evaluated by God.*

To pray, "let it be ratified in heaven," then, is to pray knowing that the full authority for authorizing the covenant resides with God. It is also to pray knowing that, as we await a world made new—our future paradise—we do God's redemptive work. We know that God is the one who determines and measures the degree of our commitment or faithfulness in doing the work.

Personal Reflection

- Do I live as though God reigns, as though God is the king of my life?
- If I am half of the equation, how must I live to have a treaty with God?

Discussion Questions

- In what ways does God prompt our actions?
- Describe how the kingdom of God is already, but not yet.
- What grade do you think God would give you for your efforts?
- Describe how you imagine a future paradise with God.
- What would you say is the main idea of this part of the prayer?

Today's Challenge:
PARADISE RESTORED

Read the passage in the box to the right from the Book of Revelation. Circle or underline the words or phrases that strike you or mean the most to you.

After you have read the verses, write a sentence or two describing what you are most looking forward to when paradise is restored.

Departing Prayer

We long for a new world in which we will dwell with you, God. We wait patiently but expectantly. In hope, we live with anticipation for a world where there is no darkness, death, or despair. Amen.

Then the angel showed me the river of life-giving water, shining like crystal, flowing from the throne of God and the Lamb through the middle of the city's main street. On each side of the river is the tree of life, which produces twelve crops of fruit, bearing its fruit each month. The tree's leaves are for the healing of the nations. There will no longer be any curse. The throne of God and the Lamb will be in it, and his servants will worship him. They will see his face, and his name will be on their foreheads. Night will be no more. They won't need the light of a lamp or the light of the sun, for the Lord God will shine on them, and they will rule forever and always.

Revelation 22:1-5

DAY TWENTY-ONE

"AMEN."

Today's Scripture Reading

"I have much more to say to you, but you can't handle it now. However, when the Spirit of Truth comes, he will guide you in all truth. He won't speak on his own, but will say whatever he hears and will proclaim to you what is to come. He will glorify me, because he will take what is mine and proclaim it to you. Everything that the Father has is mine. That's why I said that the Spirit takes what is mine and will proclaim it to you. Soon you won't be able to see me; soon after that, you will see me."

Some of Jesus' disciples said to each other, "What does he mean: 'Soon you won't see me, and soon after that you will see me' and 'Because I'm going to the Father'? What does he mean by 'soon'? We don't understand what he's talking about."

Jesus knew they wanted to ask him, so he said, "Are you trying to find out from each other what I meant when I said, 'Soon you won't see me, and soon after that you will see me'? I assure you that you will cry and lament, and the world will be happy. You will be sorrowful, but your sorrow will turn into joy. When a woman gives birth, she has pain because her time has come. But when the child is born, she no longer remembers her distress because of her joy that a child has been born into the world. In the same way, you have sorrow now; but I will see you again, and you will be overjoyed. No one takes away your joy. In that day, you won't ask me anything. I assure you that the Father will give you whatever you ask in my name. Up to now, you have asked nothing in my name. Ask and you will receive so that your joy will be complete."

John 16:12-24

125

Reflection

Congratulations; you made it to the final day of the challenge! I'm thrilled for you to have made your way through the Wesley Covenant Prayer. Take a moment to say aloud, "Amen!" "Amen" means, "Yes, indeed!" or "Surely . . . in very truth!" To say, "Amen," in the Wesley prayer is essentially to say that you confirm that what has been said is indeed the desire of your heart and that you will strive to make it true. You have the ability to make it so through the power of the Holy Spirit.

Let's take this final day to summarize where we've been as we have navigated this challenge. First, we discussed various aspects of the prayer related to surrender and suffering. I believe God's will is for the world to be made whole. God's way of making the world whole is through the death, burial, resurrection, and ascension of Jesus. To faithfully participate with God in God's mission to restore the world toward its intended wholeness, as we imitate the life and ministry of Jesus, is to surrender. When we surrender, we let go of the often deep-seated desires to control our own lives and, instead, give way to God's intentions for our lives and for the world.

Giving way is not giving up. Giving way is the intentional decision we make every day to lay aside our own will and take on God's will. To give up is simply to quit. Obviously, Wesley does not intend for Christians to quit. Wesley intends for Christians to seek first God's will by becoming completely devoted to God's mission.

To suffer is to open ourselves to God's will, even if it means it costs us something and causes us to experience difficulties and discomfort. Deeply committed disciples know that when we surrender to God's will, we open the door to the possibility of suffering. Disciples of Jesus choose to proceed with participating in God's mission, especially for the benefit of others, even though suffering might be inevitable and necessary.

Second, we discussed how the second part of the prayer might mean that we are honored or made humble. Participating with God's mission might very well mean that we are admired for our ministry in some way or we might even be made to feel small or insignificant. Deeply committed disciples of Jesus are fully aware that faithful participation might mean appreciation and approval, or it might mean that our ministry is seen as inconsequential. However, committed disciples choose to faithfully participate in God's mission anyway.

> *Together, in community, we commit to who matters and we commit to what matters.*

Lastly, we discussed community and commitment. Essentially, community is fellowship and friendship. Fellowship and friendship are formed because of the similar values, beliefs, and interests we share with one another. The result of connecting with others who share our values, beliefs, and interests, regardless of the size of the group, produces a desire to share life together. Commitment is an anticipated outcome of a community that cares for and is attentive to the needs of others within the group. Loyalty, devotion, and ultimately, love, are the benefits of a healthy community. We are faithful to those with whom we share a common purpose, and it can be understood that our level of commitment is directly tied to the fellowship and friendship of the community we experience. Together, in community, we commit to *who* matters and we commit to *what* matters. "Amen!"

Personal Reflection

- Will I continue to live out the principles and precepts of this prayer? How?
- How will I stay in tune to the Holy Spirit?

Group Discussion

- What three principles or precepts from this prayer will you remember the most?

Today's Challenge:

ENDORSE AND ENCOURAGE

Give this book to a friend or another group so they might also share in the joy of living a life in alignment with the Wesley Covenant Prayer. Take this challenge to another level by committing to lead a person or group through this book.

- Are you excited, scared, or both to live more fully into this challenge?
- How might this group stay together?
- How do we help measure one another's faithfulness?
- What would you say is the main idea of this part of the prayer?

Departing Prayer

God, grant us the ability to live out this prayer every day of our lives. May we honor you, O God, as we seek to humbly represent you on this earth. As we surrender, even to the point of suffering, we pray that your name would be known and made great. Remind us daily, O God, of the relationship you long to have with all your children of the earth. Find us faithful in our daily commitment, we pray. Amen.